CHRISTMAS

CHRISTMAS
Theological Anticipations

BY
Adam C. English

CASCADE *Books* · Eugene, Oregon

CHRISTMAS
Theological Anticipations

Cascade Books
An Imprint of Wipf and Stock Publishers
199 W. 8th Ave., Suite 3
Eugene, OR 97401

www.wipfandstock.com

PAPERBACK ISBN: 978-1-4982-3932-5
HARDCOVER ISBN: 978-1-4982-3934-9
EBOOK ISBN: 978-1-4982-3933-2

Cataloguing-in-Publication data:

Names: English, Adam C.

Title: Christmas : theological anticipations / Adam C. English.

Description: Eugene, OR: Cascade Books, 2016 | Includes bibliographical references.

Identifiers: ISBN 978-1-4982-3932-5 (paperback) | ISBN 978-1-4982-3934-9 (hardcover) | ISBN 978-1-4982-3933-2 (ebook)

Subjects: LCSH: 1. Christmas. | 2. Theology | 3. History | 4. Manners and customs. | 5. Title.

Classification: GT4986.A1 E50 2016 (paperback) | GT4986.A1 (ebook)

Manufactured in the USA   10/07/16

Contents

Acknowledgments

THE SPIRIT OF CHRISTMAS is the spirit of thankfulness. I am thankful to many people and I will name a few, starting with Father Joseph Marquis of the St. Nicholas Institute, Mrs. Carol Myers of the St. Nicholas Center, and Father Gerardo Cioffari of the Centro Studi Nicolaiani. I am grateful for the encouragement of my colleagues in the Department of Christian Studies, the College of Arts and Sciences, the Divinity School, and Wiggins Library at Campbell University, with special thanks to the college's associate dean, Dr. Glenn Jonas, my dean, Dr. Mike Wells, my provost, Dr. Mark Hammond, Campbell's president, Dr. Brad Creed, and chancellor, Dr. Jerry Wallace. A word of gratitude is in order to the editorial staff at Wipf and Stock. I could not imagine my life without the support of Charissa, W.D., Nancy and Dan, my siblings, and my wife's wonderful family who love me and whom I love dearly.

I dedicate this book to the future: Cassidy, Rachel, Rebekah, Iain, Brett, Aubryn, Braylon, Caden, Jessica, Makayla, Kaitlyn, Weston, Colton, Colten, Zachary, Lizzy, Ellie, Nate, Mary-Haven, Teagan, Miles, Amos, Kara, Jade, Elle, Hanna, Hannah, Gracie, Mariah, Thomas, Summer, Angelica, Chadisey, Winter, Autumn, Elizabeth, Catherine, Madison, Katy, Brady, Adam, Emilee, Eliza, Liam, Aaron, Isaac, Natalie, Allison, Alyssa, Hannah, Emma, Drew, Blake, Bennett, Michala, Eva Gray, Izzy, Lee, John Duncan, Hayden, Abby, Emily . . .

Santa Claus in Bethlehem

IT'S THE MOST MUSICAL time of the year. Church choirs carol door to door in the frosty night air. Families gather round the piano and sing while sipping eggnog. Pop artists shamelessly cash in on the easy money of a holiday album. Perry Como, Frank Sinatra, Elvis Presley, Linda Ronstadt, The Beach Boys, The Jackson 5, Barbra Streisand, Neil Diamond, Mariah Carey, NSYNC, Michael Bublé, Kelly Clarkson, Taylor Swift, Justin Bieber . . . you get the picture. Seasonal standards dominate the airwaves. More than a few radio stations switch over to an endless rotation of holiday hits. Deeply pious cantatas blend seamlessly with catchy jingles. The stand-up Hallelujah chorus from Handel's *Messiah* follows Elmo and Patsy's beer tab-twanged "Grandma Got Run Over by a Reindeer" on the radio and we all feel the swell of the season.

Holiday music sounds off in miniature the eclecticism at work in the larger culture. December witnesses high art pressed into plastic yard ornaments and low art elevated to city hall decoration. A Hanukah menorah hangs next to a North Pole elf on the Christmas tree and no one thinks anything of it. In neighborhood drive-through light displays, ancient Jewish, modern American, and medieval Bavarian traditions collide and comingle like old friends. Christmastime welcomes a kaleidoscope of nostalgic, religious, and kitschy stuff. Bronner's Christmas Wonderland wonderfully demonstrates this fact.

Located in the well-groomed and tourist-friendly Bavarian town of Frankenmuth, Michigan, Bronner's Christmas Wonderland draws over two million visitors a year to view the inventory of tree ornaments and Christmas trimmings, making it one of the top attractions in the state.

Sprinkled around the parking lot perimeter are an assortment of nativity sets with life-sized figures of Mary and Joseph, all being watched over by three seventeen-foot–tall Santas and a snowman. At the far end of the lot visitors can enter an exact replica of the Chapel from Oberndorf, Austria where pastor Joseph Mohr and musician Franz Xavier Gruber first performed "Silent Night" in 1818. Inside the main store, visitors discover a winter warehouse of personalize-able ornaments, nativity displays, and other holiday home décor. Bronner's Christmas Wonderland stirs powerful emotions for bygone days of childhood play, heartfelt religious devotion, and family. It feeds the instinctual desire to "nest" the home with colorful decorations. And the devout Lutheran faith of the Bronner family infuses everything. The store has consistently displayed and promoted its motto: "Enjoy CHRISTmas, It's HIS Birthday; Enjoy Life, It's HIS Way." Such a place channels and magnifies the cultural, spiritual, and personal meanings and emotions of Christmas.

Seen from another angle, the town of Frankenmuth and its beloved Bronner's Christmas Wonderland exemplify one of the key characteristics of these postmodern times you and I live in: bricolage. The term *bricolage* names the untidy habit of grouping all kinds of different things into the same experience. Bricolage refers to the process of cutting, lifting, and pasting to create something novel. Think of an art collage where magazine pictures of cars, perfume, dogs, and celebrities get clipped and glued together with beads, string, and candy to create one conglomerate picture—this is life as we know it: a pastiche of parts. The touristy town of Frankenmuth comingles Bavarian architecture, deep-fried chicken, mega-shopping, and yesteryear tourism. What is astounding is that this gonzo mishmash of styles and experiences does not discombobulate our innards or make our heads spin. It sits perfectly well with our other life expectations. We have come to expect life and all its pieces to get cobbled together from many sources—some ancestral, some cultural, some commercial, some religious.

Those of us who have since our youth breathed the air of postmodernity (whether we called it by that name or not) have acquired a taste for the bric-a-brac Christmas with its family meals, crass sweaters, and inflatable snowmen in the yard. Like an Internet web search that displays anything and everything, so the holidays have a way of summoning the bonkers and the beautiful, the neon blitz of the shopping mall and the gentle wonder of midnight Mass.

It may come as a surprise, but I do not intend here to reject the hodge-podge of the season in favor of some idealized purity. The allure of Advent for me as a theologian is that it combines the high and holy with the popular and preposterous. On Christmas Eve kids gather around granddad's knees to hear the birth story from Luke 2 and "'Twas the Night Before Christmas." What can this mean?

In this book I want to take into account the rich theological and biblical themes of the season as well as family traditions, carols, legends, and lore. I plan to excavate the theology of the incarnation but also entertain the many expressions of holiday spirit and festive cheer that attend it. I hope not to leave anything out but include the silly with the serious and the featherweight with the ponderous—just as it actually happens at Christmastime.

Christmas brims with anticipation.

Framing the Manger

The Bible sketches the holy nativity scene in sparse and iconic prose while gathering together a truly eclectic cast of characters. Mother and father, angels and shepherds, farm animals, wise men, and ordinary townspeople clump and conglomerate around the manger. The manger represents bricolage in action. We see a microcosm of the church and of the wide-ranging kinds of members who make up each local congregation in the body of Christ. Each character in the biblical story in some way represents each of us—the community of faithful believers who carry on the story today.

Let us take a peek at the actors in this company.

At the center lies the Christ child, meek and mild. In some ways he is easily overshadowed by everyone else in the frame, but if we keep our eyes on him, if we keep moving toward him, if we keep him at the heart of worship, all else will come into focus. And here especially is where we might learn from the example of children. Children pay particular attention to the baby Jesus. In the living room display sets, it is the baby Jesus figurine that is most often swiped by toddlers and preschoolers. Straining on tippy toes, pudgy little fingers feel around until they grasp the baby and then carry him off to other play sets and other adventures. Martin Luther (1483–1546) once complained about his theology students, saying that he wished he could get them to pray the way his dogs went after meat. He might well wish the Christians of today would strain and grasp for Jesus the way toddlers do.

If we peer in at the infant asleep in the manger, what will we see? Not all see with the same eye, but for those who can see, there is a vision of greatness tucked away in the smallness of the crib. In a sermon delivered by Ælred of Rievaulx (1109–1167) we find this lilting passage about the Son of God in the manger.

> He bends himself down so that he might raise us up not only from the sin into which we had fallen but also from the penalty of sin to which he has descended. Therefore, the beginning of our salvation is there in the spectacle of his humility. Therefore, let us see our Lord first of all in this humility, in this littleness, in this poverty. And who is there who cannot see him in all these things? Now through the whole world it is known that God was made human (Ps 75:2; Mal 1:11), a little human, and a poor human. But not all see him with the same eye.[1]

What strikes Ælred more than anything is the littleness, humility, and poverty of the infant King, the lowly Lord of heaven and earth—a babe wrapped in swaddling clothes. Most basically, of course, the clothes should signal to us that the infant Jesus has been cared for. He has been diapered and bundled for warmth. It is a simple detail, but one that communicates love and tenderness on the part of Mary and Joseph. Luther sees theological significance in addition: "the cloths are nothing but Holy Scripture, in which Christian truth lies wrapped up."[2] How does God package his Word and message? In Scripture. What is bundled within the folds of Scripture? Jesus Christ.

If we step back from the manger crib we might take note of the angels. We must not forget the angels, even though their translucent bodies tend to fade in and out of view. Are they part of our world or not? Are they ever-present or do they only make intermittent appearances? They seem always to be in transition between this world and the next.

They come bearing news. What does the angels' announcement sound like? Like a scream or a growl or a bark? No. It sounds like laughter—"joy to the world!" And indeed, the angelic beings who crowd around the birth stall remind us that the work of Christian living should be marked by joy and happiness. They also remind us that our work is not ours alone; we never operate by ourselves. A cloud of witnesses surrounds us. The ministering

---

1. Ælred, "Sermon 30," in "Two Sermons," 87.
2. Luther, *Sermons II*, 21.

4

angels of God watch and rejoice over the one sinner who repents. They remind us that in our acts of mercy, earth and heaven join hands.

Who else appears in this portentous scene besides the Christ child and the angels? There is the blessed mother Mary who said yes to the angel Gabriel's announcement, and the kindly Joseph who stayed with her on that long night. Even as we look to the child we cannot quite take our eyes off Mary. Neither can Joseph. I imagine Joseph stealing looks at his wife, amazed, as if seeing her for the first time. In wonder he ponders her just as she ponders in her heart the soft-skinned infant in her arms.

At the very least, the presence of Mary and Joseph at the nativity scene reminds us that in every church there are those who bear Christ to us and become for us our spiritual mothers and spiritual fathers, the rocks of faith and boulders of prayer.

In every congregation you will find a few wise men who come from the east bearing gifts, as it were. In every church God provides individual members with gifts, musical talents, financial support, and leadership qualities that can be used for the good of the kingdom and the spreading of the good news. The magi honor the newborn king with gifts. Scripture records three and so tradition has assumed that there were three magi. Ephrem the Syrian (303–373) observes that the gifts of gold, frankincense, and myrrh—at one time revered and worshipped in themselves as the material representations of the gods—submit themselves to the Christ in worship and adoration.[3] What was once worshiped now worships the one worthy of worship. In these gifts we also find theological surprises: the gold stands for Christ's kingly status, the aroma of frankincense reminds us of his priestly sacrificial duty, and the myrrh to prepare the body that will one day die.[4]

Then there were the shepherds. Commentator Raymond Brown informs us that "Shepherd's Field" was located about two miles outside of Bethlehem.[5] Much has been made of the shepherds in biblical commentaries because they represent the lower strata of society.[6] They are the unsavory, disreputable, and often forgotten types. They have no impressive gifts of gold to present. They have no wisdom to impart. What can it mean that the angelic announcement of the newborn Messiah came first to them? "They

3. Ephrem, *Hymns*, 22.26–28, p. 183.

4. Luther, *Sermons II*, 278.

5. Brown, *Messiah*, 401.

6. Whether or not they were a despised class of society in the first century, as is sometimes said, is a matter of debate. Bailey, *Good Shepherd*, 33–65.

represent all the lowly ones who lead a poor, despised, unostentatious life on earth and live under the open sky, subject to God. They are ready to receive the gospel."[7] What impressed Martin Luther most about them was that, upon the sanctifying sight of the Christ child, the shepherds did not drop their shepherds' crooks, put on the cowl, and become monks.[8] Rather, they returned to their flocks; they remained responsible to the ordinary demands of family and job, but with a new light and wonder and hope in their hearts.

Churches would not exist without sheep herders, the ordinary Joes and Marthas who take care of their families, work responsibly and loyally in the different ministries of the church. The kingdom of God is made up of shepherds like these who have looked on the Lord Jesus and carry the good news into the most mundane of places, the most necessary of places.

And the animals! They presented themselves as best they could. The little carol "Good Christian Men Rejoice" reminds us that ox and ass bowed before the manger too. It also reminds us that in every church there are some oxen and the occasional . . . ass. We must learn to live and work and partner in ministry with all kinds of human beings, even those that bray and snort. Saint Augustine (354–430) interpreted the ox and donkey as the two peoples of God, the Jews and Gentiles. He counseled his congregation in a sermon not to be ashamed of being the Lord's donkey, saying, "Let the Lord sit upon us, and take us wherever he wants. We're his mount, we're going to Jerusalem. With him seated on us we aren't weighed down, but lifted up; with him guiding us, we can't go wrong."[9] Saint Francis of Assisi (1182–1226), making a more literal application of the lesson, recommended caretakers give their livestock, especially the oxen and donkeys, extra helpings of hay and grain at Christmas for their role in the holy drama of the incarnation. All creation should celebrate the coming of the King.

Mr. Claus's Ministry

I have had the joy and privilege of devoting some of my professional career to studying the biographical evidence for the life of Saint Nicholas of Myra (c. 260–333). One unexpected surprise to come out of my research has nothing to do with the historical facts I learned. It was the people I met.

7. Luther, *Sermons II*, 25.

8. Ibid., 37.

9. Augustine, Sermon 189, *Sermons III/6*, 36.

I discovered Saint Nicholas has fans. Some of his fans are deeply spiritual and pious, some style themselves as collectors of old toys and memorabilia, some are just obsessed with all things Christmas. And something else I learned—how many men devote their post-retirement lives to playing the role of Santa Claus, certainly more than enough to staff a North Pole workshop. Many Santa Clauses commit to a year-round beard, red suspenders, and an all-around red, white, and green wardrobe.

More than a few of these men fell into the role of Santa Claus by accident. Some have always worn beards and find one day that those beards have turned white with age. Suddenly their grandkids and random strangers begin greeting them as Santa. Some put on the red suit and funny hat as a hobby, some treat it as a part-time seasonal job, others just love the holiday season. One military veteran was asked by a friend if he would help out in a pinch by coming onto the base and meeting with the families and children of deployed soldiers. The heart-warming response of the children at the appearance of Santa touched him deeply. So, he volunteered to appear again the following year. Before long, he bought his own suit, grew a beard, met with area Santa groups, and had more requests in a season than he could fill. And yes, in case you wondered, down in Coral Gables, Florida, there is an official Santa Color Guard—a battalion of Santas clad in red, white, and green camouflage pants.

One man, Jay from Kentucky, suffered a life-threatening car accident with his wife. He stayed in the hospital over two weeks recovering while his wife lay in a coma. To this day she has residual health issues from the trauma. As Jay convalesced, he neglected to shave. A fine white beard grew. He walked the hospital halls for exercise and came upon a cancer wing full of children. Young kids in much worse condition than him would poke their faces out of their rooms and ask if he was Santa Claus. Jay realized that God had hand-delivered him a ministry, practically gift-wrapped with a bow on top. All Jay had to do was accept this new calling and play the part.

He visits children's wards regularly dressed as Santa Claus. One time a little girl sat on his lap and when he asked what she wanted for Christmas, she answered, "I want a new eye." Jay spoke honestly with the child. He told her he could not promise that she would have a new eye for Christmas, but he promised that he would pray for her.

The next day he went back to the hospital and the mother of the girl found him and asked, "Do you remember my little girl?"

"Yes, of course."

"You made her day yesterday. She said, 'Mama, Santa Claus is praying for me.'"

And then there is Father Joseph Marquis. A tall and barrel-chested priest in the Byzantine rite Catholic Church, Father Joseph has a well-groomed beard and a voice deep as a gravel truck. He has accumulated over forty years of experience portraying the character of Santa Claus. When he changes out of his black, clerical garb and into his custom fit and embroidered Santa suit, white gloves, and wide black leather belt, he makes the transformation complete.

He got a phone call one morning in June from a man who said his granddaughter, Angela, was dying of leukemia. She had always loved Christmas and probably would not live to see another one. Would it be possible for her to receive a visit from Santa Claus? Father Joseph agreed on two conditions: first, that the grandfather would drive him, since it is hard to steer a vehicle in a full Santa suit, and second, that the grandfather would clear his visit with the hospital—he did not know how the hospital staff might react to a man dressed as Santa in mid-summer walking through their halls unannounced.

The appointed day was one of those sweltering June days over ninety degrees. The grandfather pulled to the curb in a pickup truck with unfortunate news: "I'm sorry to tell you, Father Joseph, but my air conditioning just went out."

Even with the windows rolled down, they roasted and sweated all the way to the hospital. They arrived and Father Joseph stepped off the elevator and into the children's ward to find that the entire floor had been decked out for Christmas: music, streamers, candy canes, and nurses dressed in green and red scrubs.

Father Joseph did not walk directly to the patient he had come to see. Santa loves all children, so Father Joseph made the rounds. To each boy he gave a button that read "Santa says I've been a good boy" and to the girls a button that read "Santa says I've been a good girl."

Eventually he made it to Angela's room. Her eyes widened with joy and she sat up in bed to meet Santa. He gave her a button and led the family in singing a few carols and songs. The grandmother decided this was the right time to give Angela a blue dress that she had sewn herself. It was a lovely dress made with loving care. The grandmother also made a little matching dress for a doll with curly blond hair. Angela squeezed the doll as Father Joseph bent down and said, "Angela, this doll is your guardian angel.

God's angels watch out over us, so whenever you see this doll, remember that God loves you and is watching over you."

Angela would cherish the day as a dream come true. Father Joseph would cherish the memory in his own way. Two weeks later, on a Saturday, Father Joseph received a phone call in his parish office. It was the grandfather. "I just wanted you to know that we buried Angela this morning. She looked so peaceful laying there with her eyes closed, her doll tucked into her arms. She wore her new blue dress and pinned to it was that button— 'Santa says I've been a good girl.'"

Father Joseph hung up the phone and sunk back into his chair. He almost succumbed to grief and despair at the tragedy of it all when a thought occurred to him: maybe, just maybe, his investment of time and money and energy into becoming Santa Claus, maybe his avocation in the ministry of Saint Nicholas, maybe his obsession with all things Christmas, maybe all of it was for Angela. Maybe it had all come about just so that he could bring a smile to this one little girl on the lonely edge of death.

Father Joseph's experience narrates the bricolage beauty of Christmas. It can come in June at a children's ward. It can combine seasonal toys and commercial decorations with the heavy blows of life and death, hope and despair. It is the place where Persian magi and unwashed shepherds duck low and gather in, where Christ is found not in his radiant glory and power, but wrapped in swaddling clothes and laying in a manger.

Instigating Word

By the year 500 BC, the decisive moments in Israel's foundational history could do no more than dust up distant memories. Abraham, Sarah, Moses, Miriam, David, and Solomon had long since entered the halls of immortal glory. The twelve tribes had risen and dissolved. Jerusalem had existed as a city for over 400 years. The major drama of the Hebrew Old Testament had fizzled out even though some of its books like Haggai, Zechariah, and Malachi were still undergoing composition.

Meanwhile, in the intellectually fertile soil of Greece's Mediterranean colonies, the first buds of philosophy began to appear. These showings initially proved fragmentary and timid, but nevertheless persistent—first appearing and retreating, then appearing again. The success of the Greeks economically, politically, and militarily had opened breathing room for the philosophically minded to stretch and inhale. We read in the pages of Herodotus the historian that the Greeks of this time sailed wine-dark seas, crossed volcanic ridges, dragged through desolate wastelands, and stumbled upon verdant oases. They discovered exotic foreigners beyond their borders and ambitious neighbors nearby. They imagined cloven-hoofed satyrs and nymphs in the woods and scaly creatures in the blue waters. The world had become an immense and strange place, and they had questions.

The first Greek philosophers obsessed over one question in particular. This single question proved as elusive as the saltwater spray off the beaches of the Aegean: the question of the *arche*, that is, the "origin," "principle," "base," or "beginning" of all things. What was the rock-bottom nature of stuff? Whatever it was, it was *arche*. Did the cosmos consist of one long chain of *this* changing into *that* and *that* turning into something else? Was there one substance for stones, another for plants and trees, one for water and another for wind, or was everything made up of the same stuff? Thales, Anaximenes, and others offered a variety of answers. Some philosophers suggested that everything was composed of *water*, which can exist in a variety of states such as gas, liquid, and solid. Others suggested that *air* compressed into rock and thinned out into clouds and could be found in everything. Each new generation offered increasingly sophisticated solutions to the problem of the *arche*. Even so, no one could have prepared for the arrival of Heraclitus.

Heraclitus worked and wrote in the coastal city of Ephesus around the year 500 BC. What remains of Heraclitus's musings can be found in canny aphorisms, clever epigrams, and curious fragments:

> It is not good for men to get all they wish.
> It is hard to fight against impulsive desire. Whatever it wants it will
>   buy at the cost of the soul.
> Nature loves to hide.
> War is the father and king of all.[1]

No wonder posterity remembered Heraclitus as "the obscure."

He took up the question of the *arche*—what is the principle and original substance within all things? But, Heraclitus thought that this was a difficult question to answer because everything seemed to be unstable and ever-changing. He pictured the universe as a tumultuous and quick-flowing river. "You cannot step into the same river twice," he said.[2] Every time someone steps into a stream, the waters are different, having moved downstream and been replaced by new waters. "All things come into being through opposition, and all are in flux, like a river."[3] The universe exists as change, flux, and disruption.

Nevertheless, above the fray and ruckus of the ever-changing river of life, Heraclitus perceived that order and unity persevere. "To those who are awake the cosmos is one, common to all; but the sleeping turn aside each into a world of his own."[4] Famously, Heraclitus was prepared to give a name to this eternally organizing principle that "steers all things through all things": he called it the *logos*.[5] The Greek term *logos* carries a wide range

1. DK 22 B110, 85, 123, 53.
2. Ibid., B 91.
3. Ibid., A1.
4. Ibid., B 89.
5. Ibid., B 41.

of meaning and can be translated a number of ways. It can refer to a "word," to the "thought" or "message" expressed by the words, to the "wisdom," "rationale," or "argument" behind the thought, to the overarching logic of the argument. For Heraclitus, *logos* pulled together all the vagrancies and contingencies of the cosmos. It gave structure to the random and boundaries to the chaos.[6]

In these fragments of Heraclitus it is easy for Christian theologians (like myself) to spy the visage of John the New Testament Gospeler. John, the most philosophical and weighty of the four Gospel writers, testifies that "in the beginning was the *logos*" and that "all things came into being through him [the *logos*], and without him not one thing came into being" (John 1:1, 3). There is correspondence between Heraclitus's philosophy of *logos* and the Gospel of John's Prologue on the Word to be sure.

New Testament scholars seriously doubt that John consulted Heraclitus or derived his ideas from Heraclitus. To find philosophical reflections on the Word and personifications of Wisdom, John needed only turn to the rich Wisdom literature of the Hebrew Bible, the rabbinic traditions of Palestine, or the writings of Philo of Alexandria.[7] Even so, an intellectual kinship exists between the obscure philosopher and the fourth Gospeler. It is as if John picked up the loose strands of Heraclitus's conjectures and pulled them across 600 years of loom work and sewed them onto their natural end: "the *logos* was made flesh and lived among us" (John 1:14).

The Chaos of John

In recent years John has undergone a major reexamination by New Testament specialists. Because the Gospel of John was written so late and because its theology is so sophisticated and developed, scholars long assumed that for those reasons it must be the least historically reliable of the Gospels. New investigations and insights have compelled biblical experts to reevaluate the authorship, date and reliability of the text.[8] More and more scholars

6. For the most part, Heraclitus believed that the organizing pattern of the cosmic *logos* would forever elude human effort and human knowledge. Even "though all things come into being in accordance with this *logos*," he recognized that people "always fail to comprehend it, both before they hear it and when they hear it for the first time." Ibid., B 1. Robinson, *Early Greek Philosophy*, 94.

7. 1 En 14:24; Wis 9:4, 18:15; Sir 15:2, 24:3, for instance. See Keener, *Gospel of John*, vol. 1, 343–63.

8. See the work of the "John, Jesus, and History" SBL group. For example, Anderson,

have reason to believe that John's gospel expresses the veritable recollections of Jesus' close friend and disciple, what he saw and heard and touched with his own hands. The Gospel itself gives evidence that its author was an eyewitness to the events and not someone removed by a hundred years or more (see John 19:35 and 21:24).

New Testament scholars previously presumed the beloved disciple John could not have written the work because he was a simple and unlettered fisherman from the Lake of Genesareth. New research shows that he and his family were probably well connected to the priestly aristocracy of Jerusalem. John's family may have been related to the high priest (John 18:15). Henri Cazelles suggests that John's father, Zebedee, served as a priest in Jerusalem but did not reside there exclusively.[9] Beyond his required presence in the city twice a year, he maintained residence in Galilee where his fishing business was located. John would have helped his father in Galilee and traveled with him to Jerusalem where he undoubtedly absorbed the knowledge, rites, and culture of the Jewish tradition. It is even possible that the "upper room" lent to Jesus and the disciples for Passover belonged to Zebedee as his Jerusalem residence.

Be that as it may, what is imperative to John's message is that the *logos* does not represent an impersonal force moving through the universe but *God himself.* The Word of God speaks the wisdom, will, and desire of God— the *arche* of all things. We tend to forget that this basic truth of Christian theology sounded radical and countercultural in its own time. The curious thing about John's pronouncement on the Word becoming flesh is how aggressively it pushed against the grain of classical culture. The Christian theology of John's gospel would have irritated first-century intellectuals. The popular trend was to elevate the status of the gods, not incarnate them. First- and second-century intellectuals criticized the gods of the old myths for being far too human. They could be captured or pitted against each other. They could lash out in fits of jealousy, give in to lustful desires, kill mortals unjustly, lie and deceive humans or each other. In other words, the deities of old lacked transcendence, omnipotence, omniscience, and in some cases, basic standards of morality. In the eyes of their critics, the gods did not need *more* humanization. If anything, they needed to become less

and Thatcher, eds., *John, Jesus, and History, vol. 2*.; Thatcher, ed. *What We Have Heard from the Beginning.*

9. Henri Cazelles, "Johannes: Ein Sohn des Zebedäus," *Internationale Katholische Zeitschrift Communio* 31 (2012), 479–84; cited in Ratzinger, *Jesus of Nazareth*, 224–25.

human, more divinized, less caught up in the traffic of human interaction and more godlike.

It is little wonder that philosophers such as Albinus of Smyrna, who lived in the mid-second century, insisted that the best and most wonderful characteristic of the highest divinity was the penchant for logic, order, reason, and system. Albinus was no Christian theologian. He represented a pre-Christian, or what today we might call *pagan*, way of thinking. He wouldn't have called himself a pagan—the word didn't yet exist. He would have said he was simply upholding traditional belief and giving intellectual clarity to cherished values. Traditional Roman and Greek belief recognized many deities and spirits but always deferred to the one high god who presided over all. The highest god was not scatterbrained and disorganized like us. He was, according to Albinus, flawless in morals and perfectly rational in mind. Albinus argued that prior to the birth of the heavens, matter moved about "chaotically and discordantly" but the highest god "brought it from disorder into the most perfect order, arranging its parts with numbers and shapes that were fitting."[10] As Albinus knew, this was the kind of divinity that people could get behind.

Amazingly, John's gospel moves in precisely the opposite direction of his philosophical contemporaries like Albinus of Smyrna. Indeed, according to John the highest deity did something completely unexpected. The divine will that revealed itself initially in the darkness before time, organizing and systematizing the universe, threw in its lot with humanity. Banging through the door like an uninvited and very rowdy party guest, the Word became flesh and pitched his tent among us.

Chaos. Good news.

Human nature itches to rein in, classify, harness, tame, command, order, control. Divine nature disrupts, discombobulates, and disperses. It trumpets a new song, notches the base of the tree with an ax and then starts swinging, splitting mother from daughter and son from father (Ps 40:3; Matt 3:10; Luke 12:52–3; Mal 4:1). The world tilts toward institutionalism, toward bureaucracy, toward paper work and filing cabinets. Such a slant favors law and order, yes, but also the banality of evil that attends it—the systematizing of advantage and disadvantage, privilege and oppression. The gift of the Word unbalances the equation and so fulfills Isaiah's prophecy of the Christ (Isa 61:1–2; Luke 4:18–9). For the prophecy heralds an anointed

---

10. Albinus, *Didaskalikos* 11, in *The Platonic Doctrines of Albinus*, 47.

one who releases captives and unbounds prisoners, one who unspins the powers and horns the year of the Lord's favor.[11]

Christianity is, in the words of Cambridge theologian John Milbank, "the religion of the obliteration of boundaries."[12] By this he means to highlight the importance of the enfleshment of the Word in Jesus Christ. For Milbank, the incarnation becomes the high-water mark of history, the grand moment in the grand narrative of God's work. "With the doctrine of the Incarnation, Christianity violates the boundary between created and creator, immanence and transcendence, humanity and God. In this way, the arch taboo grounding all the others is broken."[13] The incarnation crosses the threshold separating creator and created, God and humanity. There is for humans a way to God because God made it. God snapped the taboo, God violated the boundary, God in Christ reached through the impenetrable curtain and rescued us.

And not only that. The Christian message places in our hands the dynamite to explode the limits "between nations, between races, between the sexes, between the household and the city, between ritual purity and impurity, between work and leisure, between days of the week, between sign and reality (in the Sacraments), between the end of time and living in time, and even between culture and nature."[14] The power of the incarnation breaks barriers and reduces walls of division to rubble. In Christ there can be found neither male nor female, slave nor free, Greek nor Jew (Gal 3:28). They dissolve, grow pale, disappear, sputter out. They are of no consequence. In the dazzling light of Christ the King of kings and Lord of lords, all other distinctions between individual persons fade to insignificance. If we have faith that the advent of Christ has flattened all obstacles between us and God, how much more has it done so between us and our fellow human beings?

---

11. Hannah's jubilant prayer over the birth of her son Samuel makes sense of the topsy-turvy logic of divine action expressed in Isaiah. Hannah exults that while the bowstrings of the mighty snap, the feeble strap on shoes for battle. While she who has given birth to many children goes about forlorn, the barren maid pops them out like corn from a popper (1 Sam 2:4–6)—"for the Lord is a God of knowledge" not of appearances or expectations or privilege. "By him actions are weighed" (1 Sam 2:3). Theologically speaking, the *logos* is the ultimate knowledge of the Lord and in it the final action weighed.

12. Milbank, *Being Reconciled*, 196.

13. Ibid., 197.

14. Ibid., 196.

But oh! How even the rubble of a wall can have the effect of a real wall in keeping us apart.

Why Flesh?

The Word stitched flesh in the person of Jesus of Nazareth. The Word did not simply go into Jesus or hover over his head; the Word became Jesus, born of Mary. It didn't have to be that way. It could have been otherwise. What entered the gray haze of the world could have taken the form of law or ordinance or thunderbolt. But instead what came was *word*, spoken *logos*—fleeting, uncatchable, unpredictable. It was nothing more or less than speech for those who have ears to listen. Pencil pushers and keyboard fingers put the spoken word on the record, reproducing every jot and tittle so that not one letter or one stroke of a letter passes. But writing offers at best a substitute, a transcript representation of speech—not speech itself. Speech happens in the moment. The moment is unrepeatable. Even when captured on video and audio, what has been caught is no longer a live speech but the archival record of a live speech. "You have heard that it was said to those of long ago . . . . But I say to you . . ." (Matt 5:21–22). In Jesus we encounter the unrepeatable Moment, the eternal Now, the persistent and insistent voice that counters every fixed law and written record—"But I say to you." Such a voice cannot be snatched, penned, or engraved in stone; it can only be heard and obeyed. And for this reason the religion known as Christianity is really nothing more than a long string of calls and responses.

But why? Why did the Word become flesh?

Just Believe

In my favorite scene from the 2003 family classic, *Elf*, Will Ferrell as Buddy the Elf tilts back his head and inhales a two-liter bottle of soda, lets out a thirty-second belch, and then exclaims at the dinner table, "Did you hear that?!" Aside from such lowbrow antics, *Elf* relates Buddy's Odyssean quest to find his father and his true home. In part, the plot involves the world's depleting supply of Christmas spirit. The depletion causes troubles for Santa Claus because his sleigh's ability to fly is powered by the spirit of belief. Thankfully, the remedy is simple. The way to reenergize the Christmas spirit and spread Christmas cheer, as it turns out, is to sing loudly for all to hear.

The crisis of Christmas magic serves as a plot device for many holiday movies. In the Tim Allen series of *The Santa Claus* movies (1994, 2002, 2006), the magic of Santa Claus comes and goes, transfers from one individual to another, and can be lost if certain contractual obligations are not met. It is always in precious supply and in peril of disappearing. In *Rise of the Guardians* (2012), North, Tooth, Jack Frost, Bunny, and other muscle-bound, tattooed, and ninja-trained holiday sprites must protect the innocent imagination and belief of children. More than bearers of glad tidings and gifts, these characters identify themselves as "guardians" who protect the magic of childhood belief. From what? From any and all threats to that magic and those beliefs. Grown-ups will surely groan at *Rise of the Guardians*' far-fetched nonsense, but the take-away message of the film is really no different than *The Santa Claus*, *Elf*, or the 1947 classic *Miracle on 34th Street*. In these and other shows, the protagonists desperately need to believe, or to get other people to believe. Believe in what? In the case of *The Polar Express* (2004), "Santa Claus." In the case of the many film adaptations of Dickens's *A Christmas Carol*, "generosity." Sometimes the main characters and the audience are asked to believe in kindness, other times in love, or imagination, or hope. What is important, though, is to *believe*. Holiday stores have noticed the trend and so sell ornaments, wall hangings, and other trinkets with the phrase "just believe" written in festively slanted cursive.

Of course, the very imperative to *believe* is itself an admission of defeat. People who carry on lives according to richly interlaced beliefs and convictions need not be cajoled on a daily basis to believe. Their very livelihoods, habits, activities, and conversations enact and display their beliefs. We might call these people religious, but it might be more accurate to call them convictional. In the absence of convictions, the Hollywood entertainment industry has stepped in, filled the void, and saturated the market with tales of belief that appeal especially to those who want so badly for their innocent childhood fairy tales to be true and for the world to be infused with a primitive magic. Denizens of modernity yearn for a purpose and a reality above and beyond the give-and-take, buy-and-sell, build-and-lose monotony of urban life. They want to believe . . . in what? It hardly matters. Just believe.

The quintessential expression of this wistful call to believe in belief appeared over a hundred years ago in the pages of the New York newspaper *The Sun*. In what has become the most reprinted editorial in history we see all the hallmark elements of a fight for innocent imagination in the face of extinction. Eight-year-old Virginia O'Hanlon wrote this inquiry: "Some of my friends say there is no Santa Claus. Papa says, 'If you see it in THE SUN it's so.'" *The Sun* responded in a famous and touching way, "Yes, Virginia, there is a Santa Claus." The response inspired a musical cantata and an Emmy-awarded TV special as well as countless translations and reprints. It should not come as a surprise that the author of the editorial, Francis Pharcellus Church, worked as the religious-affairs reporter for the paper. In the late-Victorian estimation of Mr. Church, Santa Claus "exists as certainly as love and generosity and devotion exist." Even if no one ever witnessed the patron of Christmas descending the chimney and even if no admissible evidence could be collected, Church concluded that this would not prove anything. "The most real things in the world are those that neither children nor men can see."[15]

Beyond Virginia's immediate question, Francis Church was responding to the ever-expanding scientific materialism and secularism of the day. At one level, the issue at stake in the editorial was Santa Claus, but at another it was the future of belief itself in the wake of "skepticism in a skeptical age."[16] Americans were at that moment feeling their traditional beliefs battered and blown about by industrialization, urbanization, commercialization, and scientific progress. "One characteristic solution," says historian Stephen Nissenbaum, "was to think that God must exist simply because people so badly needed Him to; without God, human life would be simply unendurable."[17] People needed God to exist because more than ever God seemed not to exist. Nissenbaum's observant insight brings us back to the movie, *Miracle on 34th Street*, with Kris Kringle in the wood-paneled courtroom, complete with objections, overrulings, and I-will-have-order-in-my-court-so-help-me-God gavel banging. In part, Nissenbaum names one reason so many people resonated (and still resonate) with *Miracle on 34th Street*: they wanted to believe. We want to believe. We just don't know how or why. So, all we can do is *just believe!* This has become the best and really the only advice we know to give to people yearning for belief in an unbelieving age.

---

15. Francis Church, "Yes, Virginia, There is a Santa Claus," *The New York Sun*, September 21, 1897. For an online reprint, see http://www.newseum.org/exhibits/online/yes-virginia/ (accessed July 28, 2015).

16. Ibid.

17. Nissenbaum, *Battle for Christmas*, 88.

Our struggle will not be in vain if we are driven back to the incarnation. We must once again rediscover the mystery of divinity made humanity and eternity made time. Let us not be distracted by the sore-scabbed Victorian *need to believe*; rather, let us turn our attention to the real issue, the *what* of belief, the *who* of faith. This we find in the incarnation.

A Word from a Classic

I will always think fondly of Athanasius's *On the Incarnation* as the first classic from Christian antiquity I read cover to cover. I was in seminary at the time and I read it over a Christmas break. Quite fitting, come to think of it. I sat on our blue couch next to a scrubby Scotch pine Christmas tree in our Fort Worth duplex's front room. My reading accomplishment was nothing to brag about—the book spans less than seventy-five pages. But the experience was transformative. As if tipping over a vase and accidentally spilling out the rich treasure of the church's theological tradition, I felt elated, delighted, and energized by the discovery of this Christian classic. I also felt a bit clownish. I was Nick Bottom from *Midsummer Night's Dream* upon the discovery that his head had changed into the head of an ass. I kept touching the long ears of my newfound sensibility. The treasure had been within my reach all along. I had suffered from what C. S. Lewis called "chronological snobbery"—the prejudicial preference for all things new and modern and shiny over against all things old and antiquated.[18] I had assumed wrongly that "more recent" meant "more insightful," "more scholarly," "more advanced"; I was guilty of presuming that novelty equaled progress. I was an ass, but at least I knew it.

Athanasius (296–373), writing in the Greek of the mid-fourth century, begins with a simple question: why did God become human? Saint Anselm of Canterbury would famously ask the same question 600 years later in his Latin dialogue *Cur Deus homo*, or *Why Did God Become Human?* Theologians ask it still today, each in his or her own language. Like a tree whose branches are laden with fruit just out of reach, Athanansius's question tempts us with delicious mysteries just beyond our grasp. And perhaps because it hangs outside the reach of nimble fingers and agile minds, we feel tempted to frustration. We might want to fold our arms and reject the whole idea of the incarnation of Christ as irrational (1 Cor 1:22–23). Because it presents us with an uncracked mystery, we dismiss

18. Lewis, "Introduction," in Athanasius, *On the Incarnation*, 6.

it as impossibility. Athanasius meditates on the arrogance of the human mind that declares out of order anything it cannot comprehend, saying, "The things which they, as men, rule out as impossible, [God] plainly shows to be possible; that which they deride as unfitting, His goodness makes most fit; and things which these wiseacres laugh at as 'human' He by His inherent might declares divine."[19]

In a tantrum of stomping and braying, we let our intellectual pride deride what it cannot grasp. We mean to mock God and religion and the folly of the gospel but we only make a mockery of ourselves. What is surprising, or should we say miraculous, is that the holy and everlasting One chooses to love and cherish us anyway. We should be nothing more than a misplaced footnote in the eternal history of God. We are the impossible and unfitted thing. The scorn we think to pour out on the gospel clings to us like tar; we end up covered in our own filth—we are the laughingstock, the wiseacres.

For all that, the Son does not laugh at us. He laughs with us.

He joins us in the "utter poverty and weakness" of the incarnation and the cross where he "quietly and hiddenly wins over the mockers and unbelievers."[20] The Son does not lead a heavenly assault on the evildoers of earth nor does he stamp his foot on high and demand submission. As Athanasius understood, he quietly wins the world over. In the hidden and unassuming way of the cross, the Son persuades, gestures, prods, and encourages until humans are made "most fit" to be declared "divine." What the Lord accomplished in miniature in Sarah's old and decidedly barren womb by bringing forth Isaac, the Hebrew man of "laughter," the incarnate Son of God accomplished for all the people of the world, turning what was laughable into a genuine source of celebration and rejoicing in heaven (Luke 15:7).

On this point Athanasius speaks with unshakable certitude. The Word of God wrapped himself in human flesh and took on the shame of the cross "out of the love and goodness of His Father, for the salvation of us."[21] By human standards, it was not proper or fitting that the Word of God assume flesh, suffer, and die. These things happened for one reason and one reason only, Athanasius says: "out of the love and goodness of His Father, for the salvation of us." And so we return to the beginning, to the *arche* whence the

---

19. Athanasius, *On the Incarnation*, 25.

20. Ibid.

21. Ibid., 26.

Father's love issued forth as Word to be heard and seen and touched and believed. And yet in point of fact there was no *arche*, only the everlasting Instant.

Admittedly we are treading on eternal things where language fails. It is not accidental that at the climactic moment in the 1965 *A Charlie Brown Christmas,* when Charlie Brown cries out in final frustration, "Isn't there anyone who knows what Christmas is all about?," Linus answers simply and without commentary by reading the words of Luke 2:8–11. Everyone gets it. The meaning is clear. The curtains fall.

In the end, when language and explanations fail, there is but one thing to say. And even this need not be said because it does not depend on us to say it. It has already been said. As the retired Cambridge theologian Nicholas Lash observes, "God does not say many things, but one. God speaks the one Word that God is and, in that one Word's utterance, all things come into being, find life and shape and history and, in due time, find fullest focus, form and flesh, in Mary's child."[22] The simple story of the Word made flesh is the utterance of all things into being—life, history, salvation.

People of the Word

This chapter is about the Word, the one Word of God, and so it must also be about words, the words of humans. Contrary to the sing-song truism, it is not true that words can never hurt us; words can hurt as much or more than sticks and stones. Morally speaking, our commitment to the Word made flesh entails our promise to watch our words and guard our mouths. It is the prayer of the psalmist that "the words of my mouth and the meditation of my heart be acceptable in your sight" (Ps 19:14). The third chapter of James marvels at the outsized carrying capacity of the human word coiled on the human tongue. Though small, the tongue can direct or destroy the whole body. Like a rudder that steers a ship, a spark that sets a whole forest ablaze, or a drop of poison that kills a living body, so the tongue jerks the body this way and that (Jas 3:2–10). Who can tame it?

Scripture warns, commands, advises, and speaks to the moral use and misuse of language—"Keep your tongue from evil, and your lips from speaking deceit" (Ps 34:13); "Death and life are in the power of the tongue, and those who love it will eat its fruits" (Prov 18:21). A handful of other related Scripture references include Deuteronomy 27:9; Psalm 12:3–4, 62:5;

22. Lash, *Holiness, Speech and Silence,* 66.

Proverbs 10:19, 12:18, 15:4, 18:21; and Ecclesiastes 3:7. The deuterocanonical book of Sirach recommends that in the same way that you might make a fence for your property and lock up your silver and gold, "so make a door and a bolt for your mouth" (Sir 28:24–25). Little wonder that the Benedictine Rule concludes it best to avoid speaking altogether. More than disallowing wicked and unedifying speech, the Rule advises monks to refrain "even from words that are good" so as to "cultivate silence."[23]

The social media age we inhabit sniffs at such prosaic and out-of-date recommendations. The technologically savvy citizen of today cannot help but smirk at the Benedictine Rule's admonition to silence and snicker at the charming sermon on holding the tongue and wonder if it will end with a finger wagging reminder to say "yes sir" and "no sir," "yes ma'am" and "no ma'am." What use is a thread-worn lesson about good manners when social media allows conversation to stream, refresh, and disappear in a continuous and ever-changing feed? Smart phones, dish, cable, Wi-Fi—these keep us instantly and perpetually connected. We find ourselves never without words to hear and see, never without updates, news alerts, and real-time opinions. Culturally we are still reeling from our own cleverness; we are trying to come to grips with our smart phone apps and find a "healthy balance" of on-the-go user-driven technology.

Christians should feel uneasy about such technological advances if for no other reason than the fact that our very religion centers around an outmoded piece of technology: the printed and bound book. The Bible defines Christian faith, practice, and existence. Come what may, the written word will always smell like home to the Christian. Christians can never succumb to the total digitalization of language. We will always be tethered by a book. Said differently, by a book we are tethered to heaven.

Christians, like Jews and Muslims, are a people of the Book. In liturgical processions, the Book of the Gospels is held high for all to see as it is carried down the nave, set in a place of honor, and greeted with a kiss. Christians take their Bibles with them to church, read them daily and memorize their verses. Scripture represents the supreme guide and source and authority for Christian belief and practice. One cannot hope to understand Christianity apart from the Bible.

While holding all this as right and true, Henri de Lubac (1896–1991), a delightfully quizzical Jesuit scholar from the twentieth century, argues

---

23. *Saint Benedict's Rule*, 6.1.

that Christians are not a people of the Book as much as a people the Word, the Word become flesh.

> Christianity is not, properly speaking, a "religion of the Book": it is a religion of the word (*Parole*)—but not uniquely nor principally of the word in written form. It is a religion of the Word (*Verbe*)—"not of a word, written and mute, but of a Word living and incarnate" (to quote St. Bernard). The Word of God is here and now, amongst us, "which we have looked upon, and our hands have handled": the Word "living and active," unique and personal, uniting and crystallizing all the words which bear it witness. Christianity is not "the biblical religion": it is the religion of Jesus Christ.[24]

More treasured than the holy Book itself is the holy revelation the Book contains. Christians answer not to the Bible but to the God of the Bible. To say that Christianity is not a biblical religion is not meant to diminish the Book but to identify its Lord and Master. Indeed, the phrase "people of the Book" came originally from Muhammed, father of Islam, not the Christian community. Christianity is a religion of Jesus Christ. Far from shrinking its scope, this confession expands the reach of Christianity worldwide. Converts do not need to learn Greek and Hebrew in order to practice faithfully. They can read the Bible in their own language and so find the Word in the words of whatever language one knows. The language of the Book can be translated into other tongues far and wide, ancient and modern. The printed medium does not dictate or limit the message. Its virtue and its value derive directly and exclusively from its Lord. Apart from and absent of the Spirit who makes the words of Scripture alive and active and sharper than a two-edged sword, we would have to admit that we hold in our hands nothing more than an archaic record of human experience and religious ideas.

What else do we hope to encounter in the Bible if not the Author of the text, the Spirit of the law, and the Word within and behind and above and in front of the words? Advent marks the beginning of the Christian year because it marks the coming of the Word.[25] We Christians have nothing

---

24. de Lubac, *Exégèse Médiévale*, II.1, 196–7. This passage translated by Andrew Louth, *Discerning the Mystery*, 101. Also see, de Lubac, "Commentaire du preamble et du chapitre I," *La revelation divine*, vol. 1, 296.

25. The four weeks of Advent in ancient symbolism stood for the four comings of God's Son: the first in the earthly body, the second in the hearts of believers, the third at the resurrection of the dead, and the fourth at the day of judgment.

to say—literally!—until we have the Word. It is to the first Word that we Christians must always return in the end.

Lord of Misrule

For us Christians, the conviction that we are people of the Word carries implications for faith, hope, and love. These three virtues should shape the very existence of the Christian even as they are themselves shaped by the person of the Word.

Faith

The virtue of faith translates into trust, believing without seeing, fidelity in the hour of despair. December presents just such a month for proving faith and testing trust. Ancient cultures marked the month in special ways. Greeks celebrated the Lenaea, a time for theater, fatty meat-roasts, and un-corking new wine. At the Lenaea, the god Dionysus experienced rebirth. Attended by dancing satyrs and nymphs, he came ready to party. Germans meanwhile hunted and feasted and spoke of Yuletide. The Irish had Wren Day. Agricultural communities rested from their farming duties, but their collective restfulness quickly turned to restlessness. The sedentary ease of the fallow season did not give rise to quiet meditations and gentle repose. It stirred a need to carouse, amuse, and let off steam.

Barrels of new beer became ready to drink in December. The first snap of chilly December weather signaled the arrival of fresh meat. The cold would preserve slaughtered meat from spoiling, and so protein became a staple of December meals, making up for the lack of vegetables and fruits during the cold months. Perhaps the oldest Roman temple on record is the Temple of Saturn, dedicated to the deity of seed and sowing whose holy day began December 17 and continued for a week of festivities.[26] During the Saturnalia, priests symbolically unchained the god so as to let him run free. Ordinary commerce was suspended as were the customary rules of behavior and decorum. Slaves might be treated as the equals of their masters, being permitted to wear their clothing and to be waited on at meal time. The plain toga could be exchanged for colorful garments reserved for

---

26. The length of the Saturnalia varied from three days to seven, depending on the edicts of the emperors, who sometimes tried to shorten the time in which courts and commerce were closed.

special occasions. The civil authorities made allowances for gambling in public places and cross-dressing. Friends visited friends and brought gifts of wax candles. Public banquets were held to honor the god. Some of these became raucous and out of control.

The Saturnalia was by far the most popular holiday of the early Romans, although the elite rich tended to endure the frivolities away from the crowds, in a private cubiculum or country estate. When spotted out of doors, the plebs expected the wealthy to shower coins and bread freely from their own hands. The poet Lucian highlights the most extreme behavior and gives us a taste of the Roman holiday: "drinking and being drunk, noise and games and dice, appointing of kings and feasting of slaves, singing naked, clapping of tremulous hands, an occasional ducking of corked faces in icy water."[27]

At first glance, the celebration of Saturnalia seems to offer a foretaste of society as it might become if all were treated equally and if money and pride lost their power. But in truth, it did not anticipate a Golden Age, it memorialized one, the *Saturnia Regna*. Instead of an age of the future, it referred to an age of the past. Fueled by nostalgia, people allowed themselves to follow Saturn's wistful gaze back to an imaginary era when equality and freedom wafted like incense through the streets, when those who had shared with those who had not, when masters needed no slaves and slaves knew no masters, and when friends did not drag each other to court. The magic of selective memory and wishful thinking took its effect on people as they nodded their heads in agreement: life was better way back when.

Christian faith leaves little space on the shelf for the musty perfume of nostalgia. Jesus Christ, the true Lord of Misrule, did not come to restore a lost kingdom or a Golden Age. In Acts 1 we encounter a puzzling little episode. Jesus had been executed but risen from the dead. He appeared alive to his overwhelmed disciples and held conversation with them. What questions might the disciples like to put to the crucified, dead, and resurrected Messiah? The wonders of heaven? The harrowing of hell? the sensation of coming back to life? Instead, in Acts 1:6 the disciples asked, "Lord, is this the time when you will restore the kingdom to Israel?" This is the best they can come up with. What an odd question! What does it mean? They seem to be asking if Jesus now intended to raise up an army, evict the Romans and the Greeks, reestablish the Davidic throne, and usher in a new Golden Age in Israel's history. Now that he had come back from the dead in power,

27. Lucian, "Saturnalia," 2, in *The Works of Lucian,* vol. 4, 108.

they wanted to know if he intended to use that power to make everything like it had been under King David. It's like they were asking, "Are you about to bring back the good old days?"

They missed the point completely.

The resurrected Lord responded that it was not for them to know or waste time with such things as the Father set by his own authority. Jesus instructed them to wait until they received the Holy Spirit in power to carry out the Gospel message first to Jerusalem and Judea, then Samaria and the ends of the earth (Acts 1:8). It was no mere kingdom of Israel that he had come to restore. "Behold," he says, "I make all things new" (Rev 21:5).

Jesus is no Saturn. He is not the God of pleasant memories but the God of things yet to come; not the God of the dead but of the living. Believers drink the cup and eat the bread of communion not simply as a way of recollecting the Lord's last meal, but of repeating it and so participating in the experience of his death and sacrifice. It is remembrance in the form of repetition and expectation. Communion does not snare the mind in nostalgia, it anticipates the heavenly banquet where we will sit at the common table of the Lord and share his bread.

Christmas faith celebrates the advent of something new, not the return to what formerly was. We must reject the notion that salvation aims to restore a spiritual, intellectual, and physical perfection lost in the fall. It is not the case that in the paradise of Eden humankind enjoyed all perfections which were then shattered and lost in the catastrophe of sin and disobedience. This picture of things makes it seem that Christ came to earth as a cosmic Plan B, an impromptu solution to fix what went unexpectedly wrong in a perfect system. Sin neither caught God unawares nor did it destroy God's creation. God created a good world and declared the creation of humankind to be very good (Gen 1:31). The fleshlings of creation stood before one another naked and innocent, not knowing good and evil, to be sure. But they were not perfect. They were innocent. Perfection comes with wisdom, and wisdom comes through the Word, and the Word came through Mary and was born and dwelt among us. Faith in the Word is trust that the one who began a good work will see it to completion, and that the same God who created us will also resurrect us and make us fit to see him face-to-face.

Hope

After faith, the virtue of hope shapes our conviction as people of the Word. In terms of hope, the season for celebrating the Word made flesh anticipates the coming of the new time when death and dying shall be no more and all flesh shall be reborn. Christmas has always been a time to look ahead toward something better, the promise of a millennial age, peace, harmony, and the end of winter. This hope is not unique to the Christians. Long ago humans of all cultures established traditions for ending the cold darkness of winter's ever-shorter days and ushering in the new year. In a preindustrialized world dependent on the slow turning of the seasons, the new year marked a true turning point. It signaled that winter would spend its strength and spring would soon slumber forward.

In addition to the Saturnalia, later Romans observed the Brumalia in order to mark the winter solstice. Like the Jewish festival of lights, Hanukkah, the Brumalia attended to the passage through the darkest day of the year and the anticipation of the end of winter. Picking up on this solar symbolism, the Emperor Aurelian added the Birthday of the Unconquered Sun to the carnival of festivities in AD 286. The Kalends of January rounded out the season of dissipation and decadence. Initially this celebration of the new year involved the humble exchange of gifts and the sharing of special meals, but by the fourth century the Kalends had become another reason to party with abandon. John Chrysostom (347–407) in a sermon "On the Kalends" described what happened at Antioch in tantalizing detail: lurid jokes and pranks, midnight dancing, processions in the forum, unmixed wine in large bowls, nocturnal feasts, and gaming in the taverns.[28] Chrysostom instructed his congregation to resist the temptation posed by such invitations to wantonness for the sake of self-control and Christian holiness. Disciples of Christ must somehow resist the urge to follow the scent of desire wherever it leads.

Yet, Chrysostom did more than shake his head "No"; he also tried to give a new perspective on feasting. The "heathen" reserved feasting for new moons and special occasions. Every day the Christian could enjoy the feast of a clean conscience and good works. Chrysostom's valiant efforts did not ultimately sway society to drop the charades of the season. The custom of gorging and drinking during the last days of December continued well into the Christian era. Over a millennium after Chrysostom's death, the

---

28. Chrysostom, *In Kalendas, Patrologia Graeca*, 48:953–62. For a comparison of the perspectives of John and Libanius, see Graf, "Fights about Festivals," 175–86.

Reverend Increase Mather and his son the Reverend Cotton Matter made their own stand against the familiar debaucheries of the season.

In a noteworthy sermon delivered on Christmas Day, 1712, the American preacher Cotton Mather (1663–1728) warned of the moral and spiritual dangers of Christmastime frolicking. For shame, people "dishonour Christ more in the Twelve Days of Christmas, than in all the twelve Months of the Year besides."[29] Mather made an appeal based on the vulnerable innocence of the children: "My Concern is now with our own Children."[30] He might well protest for the sake of the children and the impressions that a liquored and debauched Christmas might make on their souls. Throughout pre-twentieth century American history, Christmas Day was punctuated—and punctured—by firecrackers and gun pops, unrehearsed songs sung loudly by ragtag gangs of boys. Gentlemen chortled at "rough jokes," convivial tavern keepers offered samples of alcohol and food free of charge, the constables made arrests for disorderly behavior. Women drunk their fill and children were served eggnog and toddies fully loaded.[31]

Here we beseech hope to enter the picture. The unspoken anxiety of many well-intentioned believers is this: is becoming a Christian the end of fun? When Jesus washes our hearts of sin, are they also washed of all color and texture and personality? The gospel commands that we live free of sin, but must we also live free of frivolity? Some Christians believe as the early Lutheran Pietists did. In a 1689 rule book for the "protection of conscience and for good order" we read: "All laughter is forbidden. . . . Joking does not please God; why then should it please you?"[32] This verdict did not originate with these long-faced ancestors. We can trace it all the way back to the 200s and the Egyptian teacher of Christian faith, Clement of Alexandria (150–215): "laughter must be kept in check."[33] He instructs us not to "laugh before all and sundry, nor in every place, nor to every one, nor about everything."[34] The early saints of the church often received praise and recognition for their mastery over emotions and their Zen-like equipoise. Rarely were they caught by surprise and never did they snort and

29. Mather, *Grace Defended*, 20.

30. Ibid.

31. Nissenbaum, *Battle for Christmas*, 261–2.

32. August Hermann Franke, "Rules for the Protection of Conscience and for Good Order in Conversation or in Society," in Erb, ed., *Pietists*, 111–12.

33. Clement, *Paedagogus* 2.5.

34. Ibid.

guffaw, cackle and hee-haw, or even, we must presume, smirk.[35] The Rule of Saint Benedict warns against "laughter that is unrestrained and raucous."[36] Thomas Aquinas (1224–1274) cautions us to avoid "inordinate laughter and inordinate joy in excessive play" as mortal sin.[37]

The caution is well-intended; prudence judges correctly that anything taken to excess, even humor, can demean and denigrate. Proverbs 25:28 says, "Like a city breached, without walls, is one who lacks self-control," and Ephesians 5:4 permits "neither filthiness, nor foolish talking, nor coarse jesting, which are not fitting." These wise words should be taken to heart. Yet we should also remember, as G. K. Chesterton (1874–1936) says, that "seriousness is not a virtue. . . . [Seriousness] flows out of men naturally; but laughter is a leap. It is easy to be heavy: hard to be light."[38] The reason that lightness is hard and laughter a leap is that they both require the person to disarm and drop guard. The person who throws back his head, opens his mouth, and laughs out loud is made vulnerable in every sense of the word: physically, emotionally, and spiritually. Only the most confident and self-assured can risk laughter—only those who have had a foretaste of eternity. Martin Luther is often quoted (at least on the Internet) as saying, "If I am not allowed to laugh in heaven, I don't want to go there." That sounds like something he would have said, and if he didn't, he should have. It's not a ham-fisted ultimatum to his heavenly hosts but an expression of the very nature and essence of heaven. It is an expression of *hope*. What else can Scripture mean when it says "he will wipe every tear from their eyes" (Isa 25:8; Rev 21:4) than that the Lord will replace those tears with an uncontainable gladness—the kind that cannot help but erupt in laughter (Isa 25:9)?

The virtue of hope contests the pseudo-seriousness of our own selves and the world. Once a person has been brought face-to-face with the ultimate concern of eternal life in the good news of Jesus Christ, the concerns

35. Severus, *Vita S. Martini* 27.1.

36. *Saint Benedict's Rule* 4.8. Benedict teaches "not to be given to empty laughter on every least occasion because: 'A fool's voice is forever raised in laughter' (Sirach 21:23)," 7.17.

37. Aquinas, *Summa Theologiae* 2.2, q. 168, a. 3. So says Moses Maimonides, *Mishneh Torah*, book 1.2, cited by Thomas: "A man shall not be full of laughter and mockery, nor sad and mournful, but joyful. Thus the wise men said: 'Laughter and levity bring about illicit sexual conduct.' They commanded that a man not be unrestrained in laughter, nor sad and mournful, but that he receive every man with a cheerful demeanor."

38. Chesterton, *Orthodoxy*, 125.

of the world lose their luster. Once a person has experienced the earth-swallowing grace of Jesus Christ, all else feels hollow. From the perspective of heaven, the affairs of earth appear as little more than the scuttling of ants. Hope would have us put things in perspective. Hope does not ask that we discard all festivities and seasonal celebrations. Hope would have us celebrate with greater purpose and fervor, knowing finally what we are celebrating and what we have yet to anticipate. The false seriousness of "serious partying" turns out to be a form of escapism in which the person escapes from the stresses of life by drinking and carousing to "forget the world," if only for a little while. Christian hope does not make merry in order to escape and forget but in order to cheer on the good and make way for the world to come.

Love

Having considered faith and hope, we now turn to love. The conviction that we are people of the Word means that we are committed to words of love and works of love. Words and works must always link arms; words are deemed lovely only if attended by works and works commend themselves to love by way of words. And so we return for a third time to the history of Christmastime revelry and make a circuitous route to Christian love by way of wassailing. The word *wassail* means more than a hot drink of spiced ale; it derives from the Anglo-Saxon expression for good health. It is to drink to someone's health and well-being. The practice provided a way of cheering good friends and honoring good neighbors. Singing accompanied wassailing. Perhaps the oldest vernacular Christmas carol preserved for us dates to the thirteenth century, the Anglo-Norman *Seignors, ore entendez à nus*. To our blushing chagrin and consternation the carol says nothing of religion but instead sings of strong drink and tipsy companions.

> Lords, by Noël and the host
> Of this mansion hear my toast—
>   Drink it well—
> Each must drain his cup of wine,
> And I the first will toss off mine:
>   Thus I advise.
> Here then I bid you all *Wassail* [*Wesseyl*]

Cursed be he who will not say, *Drinkhail [Drincheyl]*![39]

The folklore scholar Clement Miles reminds us that the word *carol* had strong secular and even pre-Christian connotations in its first usages. "In twelfth-century France it was used to describe the amorous song-dance that hailed the coming of spring; in Italian it meant a ring- or song-dance; while for the English writers from the thirteenth to the sixteenth century it was used chiefly of singing joined with dancing."[40] The tradition of caroling, dancing, imbibing, and carousing spread far and wide. Troops of young men and boys would go house to house at night singing, stamping, and playing instruments with the brash expectation that hearers would pay them for their performances. Robert Herrick preserved this wassail song from the mid-seventeenth century:

> Come bring, with a noise,
>
> My merrie, merrie boys,
>
> The Christmas log to the firing;
>
> While my good dame she
>
> Bids ye all be free
>
> And drink to your heart's desiring.[41]

Unlike the lacy carols of today, the wassail songs of yore were flagrantly unreligious. Unlike the church choirs of today, the roving wassailers were rascally and unpredictable. Nor did they confine themselves to the one day of Christmas, but roamed throughout the season.

Youngsters in early modern and pre-World War Europe viewed every special day of the season as a chance to cruise the streets, sing, drink, and ask for handouts, whether "soul-cakes" on All Soul's, November 1, St. Martin's goose and horseshoe pastries known as Martin's horns on November 11, or coins on St. Catherine's Day, November 25. The practice went by many names: thomasing (after St. Thomas's Day, December 21), clemencing (after St. Clement's Day, November 23), mumming, a-mumping, and a-gooding. Rovers knocked on doors with rods (a *gerte*), threw lentils and peas at the windows, and bellowed loudly to get attention and to get someone to open up the house or the shop. They sang and danced and held

---

39. Translated by F. Douce and quoted in Miles, *Christmas in Ritual and Tradition*, 36.

40. Ibid., 47.

41. Quoted from Nissenbaum, *Battle for Christmas*, 9.

out hands and tin cups for money and if not money, ale, and if not drink, victuals. The residents of southern Germany came to dub this time of year *Knöpflinsnächte*, the "Knocking Nights." Carousers incorporated the demand for payment into their song.

> If you haven't got a penny, a ha'penny will do;
>
> If you haven't got a ha'penny, then God bless you!

Along the coast of North Carolina in the early 1800s, it became custom among slaves to perform a similar routine at Christmastide. The so-called "John Canoe" bands of men dressed elaborately, went to the doors of white citizens performing song and dance, and expected payment in return. There is some connection between the John Canoe bands of the 1800s and the Afro-Caribbean Junkanoo processional bands of today.

Former slave Harriet Jacobs recorded the words of blessing and good fortune bestowed on those who contributed freely as well as the tongue-in-cheek response to any individual too stingy to donate:

> Poor massa, so dey say;
>
> Down in de heel, so dey say;
>
> Got no money, so dey say;
>
> Not one shillin, so dey say;
>
> God A'mighty bress you, so dey say.[42]

In the "so dey say" one should hear the sounds of freedom and dissent. The John Canoe bands used and subverted the traditional forms of wassailing and thomasing as vehicles for subtle protest. In the same way, one should hear in the "God bless you" of the two tunes quoted above a clang of sarcasm and feigned piety. The ironic blessing appears in both the traditional wassailing song of the British and the John Canoe songs of North Carolina as a barb. The miserly listener who refused to give should feel the sharp stab of shame and chastisement.

Love sometimes needs a prod and a push. Love sometimes needs to be put on the spot. And when push comes to shove, love sometimes needs the shame of youthful catcalls. The lesson of the wassailers is the lesson of accountability for words and deeds of love.

---

42. Jacobs, *Incidents in the Life*, 180. Cited in Nissenbaum, *Battle for Christmas*, 289. See also Restad, *Christmas in America*, 75–91.

The Breath of Heaven

THE STORY OF CHRISTMAS does not begin in Bethlehem with songs of angels, shepherds, and wise men. We must at least go back to the conception of our Lord in the womb of Mary months earlier. As we learn, this event occurs during the sixth month of Elizabeth's pregnancy with the baby John, Jesus' cousin. And so, it is a story of conception within a story of pregnancy. One effect of this narrative setting is to remind us of the human dimension. The reader feels pulled down from the lofty heights of heaven and into the nursery. We find to our surprise and delight that the nursery is replete with theological mystery and spiritual truth. The enigma of the incarnation begins with the fact that for nine months the eternal and omnipotent Son of the living God curled up and gestated in the watery silence of the womb. In absolute helplessness and vulnerability he remained inside Mary and so identified with the tender beginnings of every human being on earth.

In addition to that, his beginning anticipates his end. As he was wrapped in the warm darkness of Mary's womb, so he would eventually be wrapped in the cold emptiness of Joseph of Arimathea's tomb. As he submitted to the fragility of the fetus, so he submitted to the destitution of death. As he laid in the quiet heartbeat rhythm of gestation, so his wrung-out body was laid on a slab of stone. And so, the Son emptied himself twice over: once to life and once to lifelessness, once to the helplessness of infanthood and once to the defenselessness of death.

For now, we return to the grand gesture by which the Word of Life submits to the womb of Mary. But first, Mary must say *Yes*.

The One They Call Mary

Our chapter opens on the famous scene known as the annunciation when the archangel Gabriel drops softly from the clouds before the unwed girl Mary to announce the child in her womb. The scene is rich with aesthetics, meanings, and deep pools of reflection. I want to consider the moment just after Gabriel has made his pronouncement "you will conceive" but before Mary has consented to it. I'm referring to the blank space between verse 37 and 38, between Gabriel's calm reminder that "with God nothing shall be impossible" (Luke 1:37, KJV) and Mary's resolution, "Behold the hand-maid of the Lord; be it unto me according to thy word" (Luke 1:38, KJV). The faithful archangel delivers his message concerning the child to be born and answers Mary's worried questions about how this could be since she is a virgin. And then there is a moment, just a brief pause in time, when everything hangs in the balance, frozen, as we await the girl's reply. This act of God will not be forced upon her. She must choose it, will it, acknowledge it, give her assent to it.

There is so much we would like to know about the setting and unfold-ing of this dramatic scene, and yet so much is left unsaid in the text. Does the annunciation take place at night, at daybreak, or in the afternoon? Does Gabriel appear to Mary in an open field or in the cramped quarters of her home? Does he stand straight-backed with wings outstretched or does he kneel before her with head bowed? Does his voice sound like the cracking of rock or like the combing of a brush through hair? Does Mary look upon her celestial visitor with calm curiosity or avert her eyes in fear? Does she answer immediately or does she take a moment of silence to weigh her response?

For me, at least, the moment of Mary's decision is captured by the perfect grace of Leonardo da Vinci's brush in his translucently painted an-nunciation on display at the Uffizi Gallery in Florence. Painted in oil and tempera on a wood panel when he was still a young apprentice, the work radiates the budding genius of da Vinci (1452–1519). The viewer feels less like someone looking at a picture and more like someone who has just stepped inside an internally lit diorama. In da Vinci's painting, the angel, who has just alighted from heaven and landed silently onto a flowery lawn, lifts his eyes from his kneeling bow to meet those of the girl. He raises his right hand in the sign of peace and poses the question. Mary, one fin-ger holding a page of text that she seems to have been reading, pulls her other hand back in surprise. But her face does not show open-mouthed shock. Neither is it giddy or girlish. She expresses wonder and composed resolution.

Bernard of Clairvaux narrates the dramatic moment:

> The angel awaits your reply, for it is time that he should return to God, Who sent him. We, too, are waiting, O Lady, for a word of mercy we, who are groaning under the sentence of condemnation. See, the price of our salvation is offered to you; if you consent, we shall at once be delivered. By the Eternal Word of God we were all created, and behold we die. By your short answer we shall be refreshed and recalled to life. Adam, with all his race Adam, a weeping exile from Paradise, implores it of you. . . . Hasten, then, O Lady, to give your answer; hasten to speak.[1]

Here is the icon of faith and grace. Gabriel announces but does not compel. God invites but does not force. We cannot say that Mary acted independently of God's Spirit. No, her pregnancy was dependent upon the work of God within her, but her response was her own. Gabriel awaits her *Yes*. Mary conceived the Word by faith in her heart before she conceived in her womb.[2] God's relationship with all of us is on display in the annunciation. As creatures, it is true, we depend upon a Creator; as children of the promise we depend upon a Father; as redeemed sinners we depend upon a Redeemer. So, in an important sense, we are never independent of God our Creator, Father, Redeemer, and Life-Giver. Nevertheless, the mystery of God's good grace is that our lives and our actions are our own. God respects the dignity of our existence.

We return to the scene. For a brief but eternal moment, all of history holds its breath for Mary's answer. Of course, the Almighty and Everlasting One could do the work of salvation without Mary. For that matter, God could do whatever God wants without any of us, but this is not God's choice. Instead, God relies upon the unreliable and depends on the undependable, so strong is God's faith and hope and love.

And what of Mary? What did she feel? Trepidation? Bewilderment? Astonishment? Gratitude? Resolution?

In the traditional depictions of Western art, the Madonna is depicted calm, composed, and placid. The focus has been on her serenity, her holiness, and her submission to the will of God. In recent years other artists

---

1. Bernard, Sermon 4: *In laudibus Virginis Matris*, "The Annunciation and the Blessed Virgin's Consent," in *Sermons of St. Bernard on Advent and Christmas*, 68.

2. Augustine, Sermo 215.4.4, *Sermons on the Liturgical Seasons*, 142–50.

have offered a much-needed corrective to this image. Take for instance Amy Grant's deeply felt and devastatingly beautiful song "Breath of Heaven." In this track from her 1992 *Home for Christmas* album, we hear the words of Mary's self-doubt and fright at the heavy load she has been asked to carry. She wonders if a wiser one should have had her place. She worries that she must walk the path alone. Her heart stretches out in hopes that the breath of heaven hold her together. In the voice of Amy Grant, Mary's prayer centers on the word "help"—first she prays for help to be strong, then she prays simply to be, and finally her prayer is stripped down to the essential plea: *help me*.[3] We must remember Mary is young and alone. She shoulders so many different emotions. Nevertheless, whatever doubts and fears flutter through her mind, she finds her sense of peace and her courage to go forward.

And so, Mary submits humbly, "let it be to me according to your word" (Luke 1:38) as a "servant of the Lord"—a phrase that is sometimes rendered more delicately as "handmaiden" of the Lord but could also be translated more bluntly as "slave." She puts herself at the Lord's disposal in complete trust—an attitude often depicted in statues and icons of Mary where she sits with rounded face framed by blue and white veil. This is the Mary who "pondered all these things in her heart" (Luke 2:19). Even if we credit Mary with unflinching faith, her resolute response to the annunciation is still surprising given her marital status.

As a young girl promised to a man but not yet married, she must know her fate teeters on a socially precarious needle. She has pledged herself to Joseph. As the husband-to-be, Joseph can exercise his rights and divorce her without recompense or explanation. Joseph, not Mary, holds the power in the relationship. It is perhaps for this reason that the Gospel of Matthew focuses on his encounter with the angel as opposed to hers. In Matthew, he is the active agent: Joseph receives the nighttime visit from the angel, Joseph marries Mary, Joseph names the child Jesus (Matt 1:18–25). But, and here is what is really surprising, it must be remembered that even in Matthew's account, God usurps Joseph's rights over the girl.[4] Before Joseph has any say in the matter, "she was found to be with child of the Holy Spirit" (Matt 1:18, RSV). The angel of the Lord only consults Joseph after the fact. And what is more, for having such a seemingly central role in the drama,

3. Amy Grant and Chris Eaton, "Breath of Heaven," *Home for Christmas* (A&M, 1992).

4. Limberis, "Mary 1," in eds. Meyers and Craven, *Women in Scripture*, 117.

he is not granted any speaking lines. We have not a single recorded word from the husband of Mary.[5] Gently then, God's Holy Spirit lays a hand on the primordial privilege of patriarchy. The unquestionable rights and prerogatives of the head of the house have been side-stepped and overshadowed. The privilege is not broken, only loosened, and only for a brief festal moment. But the moment is divine, after all. The crack in male privilege is almost imperceptible, but it is there. By God's grace it will grow.

But for now, we need to return to Mary. Can we get closer to her thoughts?

In March of 2004 a very unlikely meeting took place between the Nobel prize-winning peace advocate Desmond Tutu and a convicted criminal seven months from his date of execution in Texas. Dominique Green had been tried and convicted for a murder that occurred during the course of a robbery in Houston. While on death row, Dominique began a correspondence and friendship with the writer Thomas Cahill and, through a serendipitous series of events, Thomas Cahill was able to arrange a meeting between Dominique Green and Archbishop Desmond Tutu.

Archbishop Tutu sat down in a tiny cubicle facing a window of thick double glass and waited for the inmate to arrive. On either side of the glass there was a telephone receiver. Through the handsets, visitor and prisoner can converse with each other. Dominique was led in shackled at his wrists and ankles. After his hands were unbound, he sat down, facing the glass and Desmond Tutu. Dominique placed his right hand against the cold, thick pane of glass, a hand that his mother had permanently scarred when she held it over a gas burner, and Archbishop Tutu followed his lead and put his own polio-weakened hand against the glass. It was the closest the two would be allowed to come. Thomas Cahill left them to their own private meeting. As he waited in the adjoining room, he heard peals of laughter and the sounds of genuine friendship and knew that these two strangers would get along just fine.

After Archbishop Tutu finished his hour-and-a-half visit with death-row inmate Dominique Green, he thanked the warden and the prison officials, and then headed across the street to St. Luke's Episcopal Church in Livingston, Texas. The church had been asked to host him for the press conference. Swarms of media and news agencies had gathered to cover the story. The church, having graciously agreed to let him hold his press conference there, in turn asked him to celebrate Eucharist. Without hesitation

---

5. I owe this insight to Hahn, *Joy to the World*, 68.

he agreed. The Bible passage assigned by the lectionary for the day of his visit narrated Gabriel's announcement to Mary of Nazareth that she was to become the mother of Jesus Christ. Speaking to the gathered congregants, reporters, and onlookers, Archbishop Tutu imagined Mary's response:

> "What? Me!! In this village you can't even scratch yourself without everybody knowing about it! You want me to be an unmarried mother? I'm a decent girl, you know. Sorry, try next door." If she had said that, we would have been up a creek. Mercifully, marvelously, Mary said, "Behold the handmaid of the Lord; be it unto me according to thy word," and the universe breathed a cosmic sigh of relief, because she made it possible for our Savior to be born.[6]

Desmond Tutu's imaginative musing reminds us that Mary could have told the messenger of the Lord "No." Indeed, she had every reason to say "No." And yet, at the risk of her respectability, her standing in Nazareth and before Joseph, she mercifully and marvelously said "Yes." Mary's yes is the model for our own responses to God's will. Her yes had moved Archbishop Tutu to say yes to the invitation to meet with a convicted criminal awaiting execution in Texas. In the face of the cold efficiency of the criminal justice system that cannot help but perpetuate the cycle of victims and offenders, the good Archbishop would have us risk as Mary risked, and be the bridge of salvation that only God's mercy can build.

Handmaiden of the Lord

A common subject of fifteenth-century Renaissance painters was the annunciation, and sometimes these artistic masters would show a ray of light shafting through a high window onto the young Mary. We look at it and see it as a spotlight drawing the viewer's eye to center stage, the submissive Mary. And it is that, but there's more. Theologically, these paintings show exactly what happens in the incarnation: just as the light passes through

---

6. Desmond Tutu, quoted in Cahill, *Saint on Death Row*, 84–85. Tutu's narrative is reminiscent of a sermon Luther once gave. Luther said,

> Notice how ordinarily and simply things take place on earth, and yet they are held in such high respect in heaven! This is what takes place on earth: there is a poor, young woman, Mary, in Nazareth. Nobody pays any attention to her, and she is considered to be one of the least significant inhabitants of the town. Nobody realizes the great wonder she is carrying (Luther, *Sermons II*, 9).

the window pane without shattering, warping, or destroying the glass, so the Spirit of God implants the holy Son in the womb of Mary without shattering her person or wrecking her body. The light comes through the other side of the window pane unaltered, so the Light of the world comes through Mary unaltered—abundantly radiant and radiating. Or, to use another comparison from the tradition of the church, on the mountain of God and in the presence of Moses the bush blazed and crackled with fire, yet was not consumed. So the Lord of heaven and earth tucked and curled into the womb of the virgin, yet the womb did not crack or explode. The Holy Spirit overshadowed this young girl upon whom the weight of God rested, and yet she lived. We step back to wonder how. Even more intriguing, *why* Mary? Why was she alone chosen from all the women in the world who ever have existed or will exist to be the mother of our Lord? Why did she receive this honor? Did she distinguish herself by her own personal holiness or was she especially designed and groomed by God for this task?

The fourteenth-century mystic, Nicolas Cabasilas, tributes Mary's own virtue and character. "The incarnation was not only the work of the Father, by His power and by His spirit, but it was also the work of the will and faith of the Virgin."[7] Bernard of Clairvaux goes one step further by saying that without virtue and humility, Mary's virginity would not have been sufficient for her to be the mother of our Lord. Eve was a virgin when she ate of the fruit and sinned, which proves that virginity is no guarantee of virtue. Mary had both virginity and humility.[8] Indeed, she was more than simply a not-yet-married girl, she was a woman after God's own heart, a model of virtue and character. For this reason it is said Mary conceived in her heart before in her womb. She had faith before she had a baby inside her. She was found by the angel to be pure and unblemished.[9] Mary proved herself to be a faithful servant of the Lord and allowed herself to be made the "mother of God."[10]

Mary did not initiate these astounding events, of course, God did. Alongside Mary's personal holiness we should pay attention to God's grace. Prior to Mary's virtue is God's decision. Is it not the case that God selected, prepared, and sanctified the vessel of the Lord for this honor? Her unique privilege as the mother of God came about by a special act of divine will

---

7. Nicolas Cabasilas, quoted in Lossky, *Mystical Theology*, 141.

8. Bernard, Homily 1.5, *Homilies in Praise of the Blessed Virgin*, 9–10.

9. Lossky, *Mystical Theology*, 140.

10. See Braaten and Jenson, eds., *Mary, Mother of God.*

for the sake of salvation history. The Holy Spirit radiated, illumined, and sanctified the soul of Mary as it did Moses's when he met the Lord God atop Mt. Sinai. Just as the blinding luminescence that glowed upon Moses's face even after he descended from the mountain was not his own, so her light was not her own. It was a reflection of the true Light. To extend this "light" imagery, we might say that if God incarnate can be called the sun of the world, then Mary is the moon. She does not generate light herself, but as a reflector of the sun she is the brightest object in the night sky.

The position of Roman Catholic communion, as expressed by *Ineffabilis Deus,* the Constitution of Pius IX proclaimed during the Advent season of 1854, is that: "the most Blessed Virgin Mary, in the first instance of her conception, by a singular privilege and grace granted by God, in view of the merits of Jesus Christ, the Savior of the human race, was preserved exempt from all stain of original sin."[11] Mary, according to the Constitution of Pius, was conceived immaculately, without the taint of sin's curse. The traditional Roman Catholic position is that Mary was born free from the sticky substance of ordinary sin and lived her life free from sin. Roman Catholics readily acknowledge that this was a special gift of divine grace to Mary.[12] The doctrine of the immaculate conception, as it is known today, can be traced back to the early church.

The Proto-Gospel of James, or *Protoevangelium,* which began to circulate in the middle of the second century, claimed that Mary was a miraculous answer to her parents' prayers for a child. Anna and Joachim "wailed and mourned" to the Lord to break the curse of barrenness that weighed so heavy upon them both.[13] Joachim fasted and prayed for forty days and nights in the wilderness while Anna wrapped herself in the clothes of mourning and wept. An angel of the Lord appeared separately to Anna and Joachim and promised them a child. In return, Anna promised the child to the Lord. And when she had finally become a mother, she hovered protectively over the infant Mary and "did not allow anything impure or unclean" to defile her.[14] Fulfilling their vow to the Lord, Mary's parents placed her at the age of three on the third step of the altar at the Temple. The toddler Mary danced and twirled about as any child would. Her parents slowly withdrew without her notice, and without looking back. The priests

---

11. *Ineffabilis Deus,* 1854, in Densinger, ed., *Enchiridion Symbolorum,* 2803.

12. *Catechism of the Catholic Church* 489, 503.

13. *Protoevangelium* 1–3.

14. *Protoevangelium* 6:1.

dedicated Mary to the Lord and reared her in the Lord's Temple. The Proto-Gospel of James suggested not only that Mary was born in a miraculous and spiritually immaculate way, but raised free from the abrasive shock of sin. She was a virgin dedicated to the house of the Lord.

Did Mary in fact grow up in the Temple? We have no direct evidence beyond the Proto-Gospel of James on this point. But, the possibility is not absurd or out of the question. Exodus 38:8 and 1 Samuel 2:22 speak of ministering women who dedicated themselves to ministry at the door of the tent of meeting. The Apocalypse of Baruch, written in the first century in Hebrew, knows about Temple virgins who weave linen and silk. And the New Testament itself sees nothing out of the ordinary about men and women keeping themselves from marriage in order to serve the Lord. The dedication of a girl like Mary to the Lord and to Temple service was not completely foreign or necessarily fabricated. Rare, yes; unheard of, no. And even if she did not live in the Temple, her close association with the priestly family of Zechariah and Elizabeth gave her access to the knowledge of the Torah and practices of Temple ritual.[15]

According to the Proto-Gospel of James, Mary's entire childhood constituted a preparation for the day that the angel of the Lord and the Holy Spirit would visit her bearing news of her mission and destiny. The Proto-Gospel does not have the authority of holy Scripture. Nevertheless, it is one of the earliest documents from Christian history after the New Testament. It shows that, from early on, Christians held the mother of the Lord in high regard and saw her as more than a minor character in the drama of redemption.

The Proto-Gospel insists that Mary's virginity was at no point violated by the Holy Spirit's gift of the Messiah in her womb. *Yes, yes,* we might say, *Mary conceived virginally, by the power of God's Spirit.* But there is more, as the Proto-Gospel makes clear. Not only did she conceive supernaturally, she delivered supernaturally. The virgin birth extends the length of the pregnancy, from conception to delivery. One of the penalties of disobedience in Eden came in the form of pain in labor and delivery, "I will greatly increase your pangs in childbearing" (Gen 3:16). Because Mary was blameless of sin and exempt from Eve's guilt, she must have given birth to Jesus in a painless and unobtrusive way.

In the classical understanding of things, the hymen sealed female virginity. If the hymen ruptured in the process of childbirth, Mary would

---

15. Hahn, *Joy to the World*, 55.

have forfeited her virginity. Therefore, the infant child passed miraculously through the wall of her womb and into the open arms of the blessed Virgin. Her "female parts" remained intact and unbreached. She who conceived by the Holy Spirit as a virgin gave birth virginally—*virginitas in partu*. This is the traditional belief of Roman Catholics and the testimony of the Proto-Gospel of James. The text reports that a midwife who had been assisting Mary came out of the Bethlehem cave and met Salome. The midwife relayed to her the miraculous news that Mary had given birth and had remained a virgin, but Salome replied, "As the Lord my God lives, if I do not insert my finger and examine her condition, I will not believe that the virgin has given birth."[16] Salome proceeded to examine the virgin and find that it was so.

Many Christians also hold that Mary remained chaste her whole life. Although neither the New Testament Gospels nor the Proto-Gospel say so explicitly, the official Roman Catholic doctrine is that she remained a virgin throughout her life. That is to say, in explicit terms, her marriage to Joseph was never consummated and so she had no children by Joseph. In the late fourth century, the scholar Jerome took the idea one step further and said that Joseph should be thought of as "the guardian rather than the husband of Mary," and that Joseph also "remained a virgin with Mary."[17] Traditional icons of the church depict Mother Mary with three stars, one on each shoulder and on her forehead, to remind viewers that she remained a virgin before, during, and after the birth of Jesus, *ante partum, in partu, et post partum*. She is venerated by millions of Christians as the Eternal Virgin.[18]

Perpetual Virginity?

Where is the scriptural evidence for the doctrine of Mary's perpetual virginity?

In the Gospels and in other parts of Scripture, the miraculous conception of Jesus is affirmed with straightforward certitude. Mary herself testified to this, asking the angel how she might conceive not knowing a man

---

16. *Protoevangelium* 19:3.

17. Jerome, *De perpetua virginitate* 19, in *Dogmatic and Polemical Works*, 38–39. Aquinas, *Summa Theologiae* 3a q. 28; q. 29, a. 1 and 2; and q. 35, a. 6.

18. She is said to be *aeiparthenos, semper virgo.* Constantinople II (553); Denzinger, ed., *Enchiridion Symbolorum*, 447; *Catechism of the Catholic Church* 499.

(Luke 1:35). The angel Gabriel answered that she would be overshadowed by the Holy Spirit. The child was from God. Jesus was born of a virgin. The Son of God entered the womb of Mary to be born, live, and die for our sakes and for our salvation. On a straightforward reading of the New Testament, it would seem that after the birth of Jesus, Mary lived out a normal marriage with Joseph, birthing other children besides. If we will discover the most robust and confident defense of perpetual virginity from the pages of Scripture, we must give our attention to the case presented by one of the most formidable biblical scholars of all time, Eusebius Sophronius Hieronymus, known to us as Saint Jerome (347–420).

Jerome was one of the first to offer a comprehensive defense of the perpetual virginity of Mary. After serving the scribal needs of the bishop of Rome and cultivating a circle of wealthy supporters, primarily noble women like Paula, Melania the Elder, Eustochium, Albina, and Marcella, Jerome departed the city of Rome in 385 as a *persona non grata*. Prickly as he was brilliant, he had won as many enemies as friends and eventually, the city of Rome could no longer tolerate him. A few years later he took up residence near Bethlehem and, funded by Paula, stayed thirty-four years, writing correspondence, commentaries, and histories. He practiced the ascetic disciplines of the desert monks of Syria, going without the luxuries of life, fine clothing, warm beds, and hearty meals. For this reason he's often depicted in works of art as bone thin, pallid, and beating his bare chest with a rock in an act of contrition. But his distance from Rome and other centers of culture and learning did not keep him out of trouble. Jerome regularly engaged in undignified theological brawls by way of letters.

He is most famously known for his translation work on the Bible. He not only produced the definitive Latin edition of the New Testament, but also the Old Testament. This was monumental because until Jerome, translations had been rendered from Greek editions of the Hebrew Scriptures, not from the Hebrew itself. Jerome diligently set to work remedying the deficiency. Not everyone appreciated his new translations. Because they differed so radically from the Old Latin editions that people knew and were used to, some clergy rejected them out of hand and accused Jerome of being a hack. Jerome took cheek from no one. Temper flaring as it did on so many occasions, he slung his whiplike pen against those "contemptible creatures" and "two-legged asses" who thought that they were made holy by knowing nothing. Jerome's verdict: if they disliked clean water then the lumbering cross-eyed beasts could drink dirty water.[19] If they did not appreciate his clean translations of Scripture, let them keep their old dirty ones.

What concerns us here, of course, is Jerome's biblical work on Mary the mother of our Lord. He had heard that back in Rome a certain teacher named Helvidius questioned the perpetual virginity of the blessed Mother Mary and so besmirched her honor. In response, Jerome unleashed his considerable furies. Helvidius, as it turns out, did not doubt the miracle of the virgin birth, only the continued sexual abstinence of Jesus' mother after his birth. To Jerome, however, who was said to have breathed his last in the cave of the Nativity with his head resting on the manger of Christ, this was bad enough. In his eyes Helvidius was a "rough boor," "barren tree," and the "most ignorant of men." Not only were his "ravings" nonsense, his writing lacked literary style, rhetorical skill, and grammatical precision. "Who thought you were worth three pence?"[20] Jerome could only hope "that he who has never learned to speak might learn at length to hold his tongue."[21] Jerome's treatise *On the Perpetual Virginity of the Blessed Mary against Helvidius* made short work of Helvidius. Many moons would pass before someone would dare venture an opinion different from Jerome's. Indeed, his analysis held sway for over one thousand years, and still does in many quarters.

We need to push aside Jerome's strident and bombastic rhetoric in order to investigate his argument. Let's start with his consideration of Matthew 1:18—"before they came together, she was found with child." The word "before" implies an "after." Matthew, so it would seem, implies that later they did come together and have conjugal relations. It makes little narrative sense to say "before they had sex" unless later in the story they had sex. How would someone who maintains a belief in Mary's lifelong sexual abstinence interpret this seemingly self-evident verse? Jerome proposes we read the "before" in Matthew's verse as if to say "before they ever had a chance to come together."[22] According to him, Matthew means that before Mary and Joseph ever had a chance to join each other physically, Mary was found with child. "The Scripture is simply pointing out what did not happen."[23] Fair enough. Jerome has a point, even if it is strained.

19. Jerome, Letter 27.1, in *Letters and Select Works,* 3.

20. Jerome, *De perpetua virginitate* 16, in *Dogmatic and Polemical Works,* 35.

21. Ibid. 1; p. 11.

22. Ibid. 4, p. 13–17.

23. Jerome, *Commentary on Matthew* 1.18, p. 63.

Next we must consider Matthew 1:25, "He knew her not till she brought forth her first-born son." Two questions from the text problematize the belief in Mary's *perpetual* virginity: what can the text mean to say that Joseph "knew her not till"? And what can it mean to call Jesus her "first-born"? With regards to the first question, Matthew 1:25 seems to suggest that after the birth of Jesus, Joseph "knew" Mary. But, Jerome asks, what might the term "knew" mean in this case? It doesn't necessarily have to be sexual knowledge since the term "often refers to factual knowledge."[24] And anyone who thinks otherwise, quips Jerome, should be ashamed of himself for having such dirty thoughts. According to Jerome's interpretation, Joseph "knew" Mary in an intellectual sense, not a sexual one. If someone were to insist that the "knowledge" here means sexual intimacy, even then Jerome has an answer. The "till" could mean an indefinite period of time and doesn't necessarily imply they ever did come together.[25] So much for the first dilemma.

As for the second question from Matthew 1:25, does "first-born" imply that there was a second or third born? Not necessarily, says Jerome. After all, even an only child could be called a firstborn child.

Granting Jerome's interpretations so far, the most significant piece of evidence has yet to be considered. The four Gospels, Acts, and the New Testament epistles speak freely of the family of Jesus and of his "brothers" and "sisters," even naming James, Joseph (or Joses), Simon, and Jude (Mark 3:20–21, 6:1–3; Matt 12:46, 13:55; Luke 8:20; John 2:12, 7:3; Acts 1:14; 1 Cor 9:5; Gal 1:19, 2:2). To give just one example, Mark 6:3 reads, "Is not this the carpenter, the son of Mary and brother of James and Joses and Judas and Simon, and are not his sisters here with us?" If Jesus had up to four brothers as well as an unspecified number of sisters, then, by implication, Mary must have given birth to other children. If this be the case, then we must conclude that she did not remain a lifelong virgin. She must have had sex. Jerome remains undaunted in the face of all this textual evidence. He counters by way of two arguments.

First, Mary had a sister also named Mary identified in John 19:25 as Mary of Clopas (or Cleophas). On first glance it would seem that Clopas is the name of her husband, and indeed the King James Version, along with New Revised Standard Version and other modern translations, call her "Mary the wife of Clopas." Jerome contends that this is a mistake. Clopas

24. Jerome, *De perpetua virginitate* 6, in *Dogmatic and Polemical Works*, 18.
25. Ibid.

was not her husband, but her father. Or if not her father, she was called Mary of Clopas "for some other reason" says Jerome.[26] The argument Jerome tries to make is that Mary (the daughter) of Clopas was wed to Alpheus, the father of the disciple James mentioned in Matthew 10:3.[27] Why would he suggest this? By making Mary's sister Mary the wife of Alpheus, Jerome can then claim that the "Mary the mother of James and Joseph" mentioned in Matthew 27:56 is none other than Mary of Clopas, wed to Alpheus.[28] As a result, Jerome is able to pronounce triumphantly that Mary the mother of Jesus is not the same person as Mary the aunt of Jesus, the mother of James and Joses. She is Mary of Clopas, the wife of Alpheus. As convenient as this solution is, it should be admitted that it is based on speculation and cannot be affirmed with certainty. Even Jerome is forced to admit as much.[29]

If Jerome's first argument leaves us scratching our heads and unconvinced, just wait! He has a second argument to offer. Jerome rebuffs the idea that Jesus had brothers by challenging the exact meaning of the term "brother." Jerome proposes that when the Scriptures mention "brothers" of the Lord they refer to relatives or close friends and not actual brothers of Jesus. Jerome bases his argument on the linguistic elasticity of the term "brother," ἀδελφὸς (adelphos). He points out that it was not reserved exclusively for blood siblings but could also be applied to other forms of blood relations. More than that, the term "brother" can be used to talk about spiritual kinship or friendship, as it is today.[30] If the "other" Mary, Mary's sister Mary and the aunt of the Lord, was indeed the mother of James and Joses / Joseph, then James and Joses were Jesus' cousins. The Gospel writers might have called them "brothers" to indicate their blood relationship with Jesus—in this case, his maternal cousins.

Jerome's interpretation is creative and admittedly plausible at some points. But it should be remembered that the word ἀδελφὸς (adelphos) most commonly and basically indicates the relation of a blood sibling. Unless there is a compelling reason to interpret the term otherwise, it should be translated "brother." The New Testament writers had other terms at

26. Ibid. 13, p. 29.

27. Ibid. 14.30, p. 31.

28. See also Mark 15:40–1 and Luke 24:10. Ibid. 13, p. 29.

29. Ibid. 14, p. 30. A simpler argument, and one made by Hegesippus, is that Clopas was the brother of Joseph. In this case, Mary the wife of Clopas would be the Virgin Mary's sister-in-law, and her children would be paternal cousins of Jesus.

30. By extension, he would undoubtedly give the same explanation for the term "sister." Ibid. 12–7, p. 27–37.

their disposal besides ἀδελφὸς that they could have used if they wished to avoid the conclusion that Jesus had blood half-brothers, as in Luke 1:36 where Elizabeth is identified as the συγγενίς (*sungenis*) of Mary, meaning a "relative" or "kin" of Mary. Furthermore, it should also be noted that other church fathers such as Tertullian in North Africa and Eusebius in Palestine were aware of Jesus' family relations.[31] That is to say, more than one church father studied the scriptural texts besides Jerome. They also understood the nuances of the word "brother" but came to the conclusion that the word referred to actual half-brothers of the Lord. That is to say, they did not all consent to the doctrine of the perpetual virginity of Mary.

The cumulative weight of the various biblical texts tips away from the conclusion that Mary was a lifelong virgin and toward the conclusion that she was not. I have deep admiration and respect for my Roman Catholic brothers and sisters, but on this point of scriptural understanding I must dissent. I confess with Christian confidence that she was a virgin before she conceived Jesus and that her conception of Jesus was virginal and miraculous, as the Scriptures testify. But the Scriptures indicate that she had other children in the normal fashion. Mary's perpetual virginity is based more on tendentious conjecture than on scriptural evidence.

Some might argue that the belief in the lifelong virginity of Mary creates a necessary theological bulwark for the divinity of Jesus. It is said by some that the believer who allows himself or herself to doubt the perpetual virginity of Mary will end up doubting the virgin birth and then the divinity of Jesus altogether. Nothing will prevent the sad soul from doubting every other historical detail. This line of thinking relies on a slippery slope argument that in my judgment amounts to a logical fallacy. Scripture gives explicit testimony to Jesus' miraculous birth and to Mary's conception prior to knowing a man. Scripture does not give evidence of lifelong and perpetual virginity any more than it gives direct evidence that she herself was born immaculate (without sin) or that she was bodily assumed into heaven before death. Not affirming the one does not necessarily lead to doubting the other. Non-consent to the doctrine of perpetual virginity does not automatically lead to, result in, or in any way infer doubt about the virgin birth.

---

31. Eusebius, *Historia Ecclesiastica* 1:7:11–4; 3:20. *The Catechism of the Catholic Church* follows Jerome's reasoning and interprets these biblical passages as referring to "cousins" or children of another Mary besides Jesus' mother, 500.

Eternity Making a New Start

We need to turn ourselves in a slightly different direction now and think about an obvious question, one that probably should have been raised sooner. What is so important about the virgin birth? Why a virgin birth at all? Why not conception in the usual way? Central to the Christian Gospel, as represented by the ancient and universally approved Apostle's Creed and the Nicene Creed, is the confession that the Lord was "born of the Virgin Mary." Not only Matthew and Luke, but the prophecy of Isaiah 7:14 provide the biblical basis for this confession.[32]

Theologically, what is at stake is not Mary's sexual activity but rather the Lord Jesus' divinity.[33] In the womb of Mary, God united divinity and humanity. The one from Nazareth is also the one from heaven, the son of man and the son of God. If Jesus had been the product of Mary and Joseph in the usual way, his divinity would have been an add-on, an extra, something external and not original to his nature. But instead the Scriptures testify to two natures, divine and human. Matthew, to offer just one example, makes this clear within the first chapter of his Gospel: the child will be Messiah (1:18), the salvation of his people from sin (1:21), Emmanuel God with us (1:23), and the man Jesus (1:25).[34] Saint Augustine preached this truth in these words: "he took to himself what he was not, while remaining what he was."[35] He came to us without departing his divinity; his power was condensed and confined in the body of a child without being withdrawn from

---

32. For a fresh consideration of the evidence by an important New Testament scholar, see Lincoln, *Born of a Virgin?*, especially 68–98 on Matthew's witness and 99–124 on Luke. Thanks to Alicia Myers for this source.

33. Indisputably, the historical arguments for the perpetual virginity of Mary have assumed a strong link between human sexuality and sin. The working hypothesis in many such arguments has been that sexual intercourse is inherently tainted with guilt and the penalty of sin. For example, Saint Leo the Great made this comment in regards to Mary: "Although no conception takes place in mothers, as a rule, without the stain of sin, this mother derived cleansing from the very source that gave her to conceive. Where the transfer of a father's seed has not penetrated, the very first onset of sin has not been introduced." Sinfulness is introduced by transfer of the father's seed. But Mary's "untouched virginity did not know concupiscence." See Sermo 22, *Sermons*, 83. Leo was not alone in his understanding of the innately sinful nature of sexual activity. Augustine shared it, as did many other church fathers, especially those who defended traducianism. See Augustine, *Enchiridion* 34.

34. Kingsbury, "The Birth Narrative of Matthew," in Aune, ed., *Matthew in Current Study*, 154–65.

35. Augustine, Sermo 184, *Sermons* III/6, 17.

the mass of the universe. A little later in the same Christmastime sermon Augustine says:

> Born of his mother, he commended this day to the ages, while born of his Father he created all ages. That birth could have no mother, while this one required no man as father. To sum up, Christ was born both of a Father and of a mother; both without a father and without a mother; of a Father as God, of a mother as man; without a mother as God, without a father as man.[36]

Augustine wishes to make clear that there are not two sonships or two sons. His eloquent sermon communicates instead the truth that the two natures of the one Son have two origins and two births: one eternal and from the Father, one temporal and from his mother. The birth of the Son in time does not take from or add to his birth in eternity.[37] These things took place for our deliverance.

Bishop Kallistos Ware, Patriarchate of Constantinople in the Orthodox Church, marks out three crisp reasons for the virgin birth:

First, the mother's virginity signals the Son's uniqueness. Though born of flesh and blood, he is not only man, he is also born of God. And so "he points always beyond his situation in space and time to his heavenly and eternal origin."[38] Christ has a dual origin, as Augustine noted above, and this is most clearly expressed in the miracle of the virgin birth.

Second, the fact that he was born of a virgin indicates that the initiative for Mary's conception was not human but divine. Ordinarily, human life starts with the sexual union of two individuals, but this life began in the heart of God.

Third, the doctrine of the virgin birth suggests that what took form in Mary's womb was not completely new. Instead, as the Gospel of John perceived, inside Mary's body the Ancient of Days took flesh. "At Christ's birth, therefore, no new person came into existence, but the pre-existent person of the Son of God now began to live according to a human as well as a divine mode of being."[39]

Ælred, the twelfth-century abbot of Rievalux in Yorkshire, marvels at "eternity making a new start, strength itself weak, bread hungry, the fountain thirsty" as he wonders before his own congregation: "But who is

36. Ibid., 18.

37. Leo, *Tomus Leonis*, in Denzinger, ed., *Enchiridion Symbolorum*, 291.

38. Ware, *Orthodox Way*, 76.

39. Ibid., 77.

49

there who would behold the beginning of our salvation, the day of human redemption, and not break forth in exultation and praise, in the sounds of feasting (Ps 41:5)?"[40] The paradox of *God with us* does not finally collapse like an accordion, nor does it break apart from the exertion of its own spinning and centripetal force. It blossoms into shouts of praise and testaments of worship. Ælred's response is just right: we should bow humbly before the unknown edge of mystery and incomprehension.

Unlike the Magic Hat

The 1969 Rankin-Bass pastel-colored classic, *Frosty the Snowman*, tells the story of a snowman rolled and shaped from a fresh snowfall by a group of children. When an old black magician's hat gets placed on top of his head, the lucky snowman springs to life. As soon as he blinks his eyes for the first time, Frosty speaks his unexpected yet fitting first words, "Happy birthday!" Fun loving and good-natured, Frosty discovers he can move, sweep, juggle, and count to ten. He exclaims he is alive and then comments, "What a neat thing to happen to a nice guy like me." He is real in every possible way, as is demonstrated by the fact that his tummy is ticklish. Have we found an appropriate—if childish—analogy for the incarnation? Is divinity like an old magic hat set upon the flesh and bones of Jesus?

In *Frosty*, the power of life resides in the hat and without the hat Frosty is just a pile of mushy snow. So in Christ, it would seem, eternal divinity is set upon the humanity of Jesus. Frosty, for the sake of the little girl Karen at the dramatic and climatic moment in the story, dissolves into a puddle and in this way loses his life. But then, after a time of mourning, Frosty gets reformed and reanimated by the hat. In the same way, it might be argued, the "magic" of God's Spirit empowers Jesus until on the cross he dies and dissolves for our sakes. His friends mourn his loss, but on the third day the "magic" returns, putting life and motion back into Jesus in the resurrection.

The so-called "four fences" of Chalcedon become helpful at this point. The Council of Chalcedon, the fourth great ecumenical council of the Church which met in the year 451, laid down the rule for speaking of the union of natures in Christ: "We confess that one and the same Christ, Lord, and only-begotten Son, is to be acknowledged in two natures without confusion, change, division, or separation."[41] In Mary's womb the human

40. Ælred, "Sermon 30," "Two Sermons," 85.

41. Council of Chalcedon (451), in Denzinger, ed., *Enchiridion Symbolorum*, 302.

nature of Jesus was not absorbed into the divine nature of Christ, nor was the divine nature partitioned off and kept separated from the human nature, nor did the two natures blur and blend into a single divino-human hybrid.[42] The "fences" around Christ specify that his natures not be confused, changed, divided, or separated.[43]

On the testimony of Scripture, we confess the virgin birth because in Mary's womb there rests the union not of male and female but of the fullness of God and the sum total of humanity. We also confess that the divine and the human united in the one person Jesus Christ but not in a way that compromised or distorted one or the other. To be sure, we are balancing on a tricky theological tightrope. What does this Word made flesh that the Chalcedonian council so persistently championed mean for our daily exercise of the faith?

To answer that question, let's pack our bags and travel to the European city of Galati, Romania. The Danube River slices through this city most notable for its steel factories. Not exactly a vacation destination. In fact, the repeating columns of drab concrete buildings match the somber mood of the overcast skies. Galati's blue-collar denizens walk to and from work with heads down, keeping to themselves. Deep within this industrial city there is a tiny oasis located in the Word Made Flesh Community Center organized by Christopher Huertz, a ministry to the poorest of the Romanian community—especially Romanian children. In the center children and adults can participate in literacy classes, computer training, counseling, and art. They receive a hot meal and can play a game of basketball on the courts.

At one end of the Word Made Flesh Community Center complex, a visitor can find a tucked-away chapel. It is a modest and unassuming building from the outside. Inside, it is a place of peace and quiet. Each morning ministry workers and members from the community begin the day with liturgy and prayer there. On the wall hangs a cross constructed from pieces of discarded scrap metal found in the neighborhood and welded together. Under the cross stands an altar and in the middle of the floor, a prayer rug. Of these fixtures, the prayer rug is the most precious. It was something that the community members themselves wanted to make, so they built a loom to weave a prayer rug, and then created on that loom a beautiful piece. It

---

42. There are many notable guides through the christological heresies. See Torrance, *Incarnation*.

43. Council of Chalcedon (451), in Denzinger, ed., *Enchiridion Symbolorum*, 301.

took nearly two years to complete the rug. It was taken off the loom and laid out lovingly on the floor of the chapel.

The Romanian sewing group who labored on the rug made for themselves a treasured memorial to their friendship and their community. In their morning sessions, seated around the rug, these Romanian Christians pray for the sick, the jobless, and the heartbroken. But there is more to the story.

The Word Made Flesh prayer rug represents more than a *monument* to prayer or a *memento* of friendship—it is an *enactment* of these things. Once a week, community members take scraps of cloth they collect from the friends they prayed for and weave those pieces of fabric into the rug. Each piece of fabric presents itself as a prayer, not just a reminder of prayer, but a prayer itself, a bit of friendship and community. As long as the community prays, it creates rug—always added to and never finished.[44]

So also, the Word made flesh in Mary's womb never quite finished incarnating, but is forever sewing new life onto the patchwork gown and veil of Christ's bride, the church. So she is adorned in beautiful and living colors to meet her groom and enter the wedding banquet of heaven on earth (Rev 21:2, 9).

44. Huertz, *Unexpected Gifts*, xxii.

On This Day

WE HAVE INHERITED FOUR Gospels in the New Testament, not just one. Isn't it curious that the early church did not choose one to be the official version and get rid of the others? What if they had felt especially creative and decided to harmonize the four accounts into one mega-Gospel? Thankfully, they didn't. The preservation of *four* Gospels has significant implications for our study of the infancy of Jesus because each Gospel begins the story of Jesus at a different point in time. Each of those beginnings illuminates something important about the incarnation and birth of our Lord.

When Jesus makes his first appearance in the New Testament's earliest Gospel, the Gospel of Mark, he steps out as a fully grown man just arrived from Nazareth of Galilee (Mark 1:9). Mark never mentions the details surrounding Mary's miraculous conception or the dramatic birth in Bethlehem. If the New Testament had preserved this Gospel alone as the single witness to the life of Jesus, we might be left with the impression that God chose Jesus unexpectedly from the crowd of people gathered by the waters of the Jordan to be adopted as the honorary son of God. Mark simply relates that Jesus came from Nazareth in Galilee and was put under water by John who was baptizing many individuals at the time. When he came up for air "he saw the heavens torn apart and the Spirit descending like a dove on him" (Mark 1:10). He heard a voice from heaven—"You are my Son, the Beloved; with you I am well pleased." Jesus went into the wilderness for a period, after which he began his ministry of teaching, preaching, and healing. From Mark we learn nothing of Jesus' birth or upbringing.

If, on the other hand, we possessed only John's gospel we would come away with a radically different impression. We might believe that God transmitted his Son to the world in the manner of the first man, Adam. John, like Mark, says nothing about swaddling clothes and cradles. Instead, he declares that the eternal and almighty Word of God "became flesh and lived among us" (John 1:14). Jesus emerges as a radiant figure in full possession of his divine aura. Similar to Mark's narrative, the Gospel of John introduces Jesus through the eyes of John the Baptizer. The baptizer looks up, sees the outline of Jesus on approach and shouts, "Here is the Lamb of God who takes away the sin of the world!" (John 1:29).

Matthew and Luke, by contrast, provide the greatest amount of information about the nativity. We could spend pages sifting through the details of their accounts. Indeed, the eminent New Testament scholar Raymond Brown managed to produce a mammoth 594-page study of Matthew and Luke's infancy narratives in the late 1970s: *The Birth of the Messiah*. We will attempt nothing as bold or laborious, but simply highlight some of the major points.[1]

Matthew's gospel opens with "the genealogy of Jesus the Messiah, the son of David, the son of Abraham" (Matt 1:1), a list of descendants organized in three groups of fourteen generations. The scrupulous record of names begins with Abraham and ends with Jesus, "who is called the Messiah," emphasizing along the way names connected to the kingly, royal lineage of David and Solomon. Although many sound foreign and downright unpronounceable to us, we must remember that the names conjured up heroic tales and mighty deeds in the minds of Matthew's readers. These were stories they knew and names they recognized. Matthew could imagine no better way to grab readers' attention than to lay out an epic roll call of names from Israel's proud history.

Matthew then relates the angelic words to Joseph given in a dream concerning the child growing in the womb of the girl to whom he is betrothed, reassuring him that Mary is indeed a virgin and that the child is from the Lord, a fulfillment of prophecy (Isa 7:14). Joseph makes Mary his wife and names the child born to her Jesus. Wise men from the east come looking for the newborn and are directed to Bethlehem where they pay homage to the child on bended knee. An angel warns Joseph in a dream to flee to Egypt and escape Herod, who has ordered the massacre of the infants under two years of age in and around Bethlehem. Matthew cites the words of the prophets for all these happenings.

---

1. For something much shorter, see Kelly, *Origins*, 1–30.

Luke gives the most detailed account of events surrounding the birth of Jesus, and for this reason Luke's version is the one usually read in homes on Christmas Eve. Luke begins with the story of Zechariah and Elizabeth. In dramatic fashion, Zechariah learns that his wife Elizabeth will soon be with child, even though "Elizabeth was barren, and both were getting on in years" (Luke 1:7).[2] Then, in the sixth month of Elizabeth's pregnancy, the young Mary receives a visit from the angel Gabriel in a town in Galilee called Nazareth. We are also told that she is engaged to a man named Joseph, a descendent of David. Mary sets out in haste to visit her relative Elizabeth in the hill country of Judea and together they share in the wonder of God's work.

Luke records a beautiful song of praise sung by Mary, known by its Latin title, the Magnificat. In it we listen to Mary's fine-spun testimony of praise, "My soul magnifies the Lord," and her salty proclamation of justice, "he has filled the hungry with good things, and sent the rich away empty" (Luke 1:46, 53). Three more months pass and Elizabeth gives birth to a boy. Zechariah names him John as the Lord has instructed and then sings his own prophetic song of praise. When the narrative returns to Mary, we find her and Joseph traveling from Nazareth to Bethlehem to be registered in accordance with the decree of Caesar Augustus. Mary goes into labor. The couple must stay the night in a shelter for animals and lay the child in a feeding trough, or as it is identified today, a little niche in the wall with a stone manger.[3] Nevertheless, the heavenly host announces the long-awaited birth in a ringing song of praise overheard by night watch shepherds.

On the eighth day the child is circumcised and given the name Jesus. Forty days after the birth, "when the time came for their purification according to the law of Moses," the family travels to the Temple in Jerusalem to present the child and to offer the requisite sacrifice of purification for Mary (Luke 2:22–4). In the Temple, the prophet Simeon picks up the child and prophesies concerning his future. Then, as if in an aside, he says to Mary that the child is destined for the falling and the rising of many in Israel and that even her soul will be pierced (Luke 2:34–5). The old prophetess Anna offers her own words of foresight and praise. Having completed the requirements of the Law, the holy family returns to Galilee and to their own town of Nazareth (Luke 2:39).

---

2 Luke spends as many verses telling about Zechariah with the angel in the temple as Matthew does telling the entire birth story of Jesus, including genealogy.

3. Maier, *First Christmas*, 44.

Later in chapter three, Luke gives his own version of the genealogical record (Luke 3:23–38). Unlike Matthew, who begins with Abraham, the founding father of the Hebrew people, Luke begins with Jesus and ends with Adam, the first man. The names in his list vary significantly from Matthew's, causing scholars to speculate that Luke means to emphasize the priestly heritage in Jesus' family line, whereas Matthew emphasizes the royal, Davidic heritage. It may also be that Matthew is recording the family line through Joseph while Luke takes the family line through Mary.[4] That fits the narrative. Matthew consistently sees events through the eyes of Joseph—it is Joseph who has dreams and Joseph who acts for the family, whereas Luke sees the same events through Mary's eyes—Mary's relatives, Zechariah and Elizabeth, Mary's encounter with the angel Gabriel, and Mary's reactions to events (for example, Luke 2:19; 2:51). Indeed, Luke most likely spent time with Mary and interviewed her at Ephesus for his account of the Gospel.[5] He records details and insights that only Mary could have supplied.

There is so much to mull over in these infancy narratives—historically, spiritually, and theologically. But we are getting ahead of ourselves. Let's start with the facts, beginning with the most basic piece of information: the date. When was he born? What year? What day? I want to spend some time with these often overlooked questions because I think we will find they contain some unexpected surprises.

The date of Jesus' birth seems obvious—December 25, as every Sunday school child knows. What year? That too seems obvious: Year One, the year of our Lord AD 1. Unfortunately, as we will see, there is nothing obvious about either of these facts. First we will consider the year, then the day.

---

4. Matthew's genealogy ends with "Jacob the father of Joseph the husband of Mary" (Matt 1:16) while Luke begins by saying, "He was the son (as was thought) of Joseph son of Heli" (Luke 3:23). Matthew clearly ends with Joseph, while Luke implies that perhaps he is tracing not Joseph "as was thought" but the true, biological line of Jesus. Scott Hahn gives a number of other plausible explanations for the discrepancies in Hahn, *Joy to the World*, 36–37.

5. Biblical evidence of this begins with John 19:26–27, where Jesus gives the disciple John care of his mother. Tradition says that John relocated to Ephesus where he continued his ministry. There is good reason to believe Mary went with him to Ephesus. Luke would have encountered her there during the journey recorded in Acts 19. Hahn also makes this connection in ibid., 15.

Anno Domini

Jesus' birth year should align with Year One. That was the working idea of a certain Scythian monk who moved from present-day Romania to Rome around the year 500. They called him Dionysius Exiguus (c. 470–544)—Exiguus being a nickname for "the Little." Although he may have been small in stature, Dionysius possessed unique intellectual and linguistic gifts. He knew the Scriptures inside and out. His friends said he was an unstumpable Bible trivia master and could answer any question they could devise. He earned his living by translating important church documents from Greek into Latin and codifying the canons of the major church councils. The reason he enters our story, however, is that he invented . . . years. That is to say, he originated the method nearly everyone in the world uses for counting years.[6]

Of course, dates, calendars, and the measurement of time had existed long before Dionysius the Bible Answer Man came along. Egyptians, Jews, Greeks, and Romans had notched the passage of time in their own ways. But, and here is the main point to make note of, time was considered by everybody to be a local affair. Nobody tracked it on a global scale. It served its immediate context and was calculated accordingly. What a strange idea to us! We think of time and date in global terms. It seems obvious to us that the whole world should be on the same calendar and clock. The only thing that should vary from one place to another is the time zone. Time and date seem to us to be a part of nature, just another fact about the world. But, of course, timekeeping is not hardwired in nature—systems of timekeeping must be artificially constructed by humans.

In the classical world, some prominent moments of shared history functioned as convenient reference points, like the foundation of Rome by Romulus (754 BC) or the reforms of Diocletian (284 AD).[7] In Roman documents, time was most often reckoned according to the annually rotating consulates of Rome (*in the year of so-and-so and so-and-so, the joint consuls of Rome*), and according to the year in the reign of the emperor (*in the third year of Hadrian,* etc.). Another way to track the passage of time was to count back through the descendants of a family line (*in the time of so-and-so, son of so-and so,* etc.). Dates could be given in relation

---

6. Mosshammer, *Easter Computus,* 5–8.

7. These two dates, the founding of Rome and the reforms of Diocletian, have not been chosen randomly. They were in fact often employed as reference points.

to recurring festivals and holy days, like the day of Pentecost or the Ides of March. Sometimes it was by some memorable event like an earthquake or plague. Calendars might follow the lunar cycles, as did that of the Jews, or the solar year, as did the Julian calendar used by the Alexandrians, or some combination of the two. The drawbacks of such unstandardized systems seem painfully obvious to us now. Besides being cumbersome, they were plagued by confusions and misinterpretations.

Even though the late classical world needed a universal dating system desperately, nobody set out to invent one, not even Dionysius Exiguus.[8] He had the more modest goal of calculating the date of Easter accurately. To this end he constructed a brain-boggling algebraic table. In the process, it became relevant to know the year of Christ's birth. Dionysius made it sound easy. In order to learn the year of the incarnation of our Lord Jesus Christ, all you need to know is the number of indiction cycles that have occurred since the birth of Christ. An indiction cycle is a fifteen-year period.[9] At the time Dionysius wrote, there had been thirty-four since Christ's birth. So, multiply fifteen and thirty-four. Then add twelve "by way of correction," that is to say that the number twelve served a constant that must be added to the formula—what is formally called an intercalation—giving Dionysius a sum total of 522.[10] To this base number, 522, you must add the indiction of the current year, that is, the number of the year within the fifteen-year cycle. The indiction year in Dionysius's case corresponded to the consulship of Probus Junior, and so he added three, giving him the result of 525 years "since the incarnation of the Lord."[11] Because the year 525 was computed directly in relation to the year of the Lord's incarnation, it could properly be called *anno Domini* 525, "the year of our Lord" 525, or simply AD 525. The

---

8. Mosshammer, *Easter Computus*, 8. According to Mosshammer, the early medieval historian Bede deserves the true credit for introducing the BC/AD system. Dionysius simply used the year of the Lord to express intervals from the incarnation whereas Bede, in his *History of the English Church and People* of 731, used Dionysius's incarnational era to frame his historical chronology. Not only did he express dates in the year of the Lord but he even referred to dates "before Christ." Mosshammer, *Easter Computus*, 31–32.

9. This is different from the 19-year lunar cycle, also used by Dionysius and, more generally, by calendars based on the rotations of the moon.

10. "Si nosse vis quotus sit annus ab incarnatione Domini nostri Jesu Christi, computa quindecies XXXIV, fiunt DX; iis semper adde XII regulares, fiunt DXXII; adde etiam indictionem anni cujus volueris, ut puta, tertiam, consulatu Probi junioris, fiunt simul anni DXXV. Isti sunt anni ab incarnatione Domini." Dionysius, *Liber de Paschate*, *Patrologia Latina* 67:453–520. See Mosshammer, *Easter Computus*, 98.

11. Ibid.

designation that would have implications beyond what Dionysius could have known or imagined.

Dionysius provided a ready-to-hand formula for determining the time elapsed since Christ's birth. But, again, he did so in order to use that number to compute something of greater significance to him: the annual occurrence of Easter. The early medieval British historian Bede (c. 672–735) was the first to recognize the importance of Dionysius's system beyond what Dionysius had imagined. Dionysius had invented—even if inadvertently and unknowingly—a Christianized keeping of time. Bede adopted and popularized the new system in his *History of the English Church and People*, written in 731. As a historian, he appreciated the need for a unified and consistent method of tracking years and took delight in the Christian orientation of that method. Writing a history of the church in England, it only made sense that dates be set from the time of Christ, the founder of the church universal. Creatively, Bede used Christ's birthday as a reference point not only for events that occurred after but even for events that occurred before it. When he mentioned the activities of Julius Caesar, for example, he located them a certain number of years after the foundation of Rome and also a certain number of years "before Christ"—BC.[12] And just like that, the AD system had a BC companion.

One consequence of the new nomenclature was to shift emphasis away from Roman, imperial markers of time and toward specifically Christian ones. For Bede, this counted as its real advantage. The focal point of history was no longer the founding of Rome, the annual consuls, or the emperors of Rome. It was the birthday of Jesus. What occurrences rank as the greatest moments in the long history of the world? What events serve as tent poles of world history? Bede insisted that the answers to these questions have nothing to do with the Roman people or their empire. Instead, from the Christian perspective, the world's story takes a cruciform shape. It folds and curves and billows according to the story of salvation as told in Scripture. The tallest and strongest tent pole of history is the incarnation of the Lord, the birth of Jesus Christ.

---

12. Eusebius, *Historia Ecclesiastica* 1.2–3. Bede's work by no means standardized the nomenclature immediately. Mosshammer shows that historians ancient, modern, and contemporary challenged the Christian computation of time. Nevertheless, the BC/AD system did enjoy nearly universal popularity and widespread usage in the West until the mid-1990s. Now, the preferred nomenclature in scholarly publications and academic circles is BCE and CE. Mosshammer, *Easter Computus*, 32–34.

And so, underpinning Bede's new chronology was a bold political and theological statement that contested the imperial dominance over time. The world does not move according to the ages of the empire, but according to the plan and purpose of God. To count from the reign of Jesus Christ rearranges more than the numbers on a timeline. It rearranges values. It declares that the new Lord of peace supersedes all other lords. In a world where, then as now, it often feels like the powers and authorities determine the course of affairs and the fate of humanity, the "year of our Lord" reminds us of a more pervasive and determinative force at work, one which ultimately disarms the rulers and authorities and makes a public spectacle of them (Col 2:15). The advent of Christ sparks a new age and a new era. In spite of all the miniature eras and ages that rise and fall on the surface like swells and waves and foam, the *anno Domini* is the bottomless ocean of water that supports them all.

There is great power and beauty in this configuration of things by which history is sectioned into the time before Christ (BC) and the time of Christ (AD). To believers it chimes a bell of assurance that the world and its times rest in God's hands. It also sounds a note of urgency to work while it is day, for night is coming when no one can work (John 9:4). This is the day that the Lord has made, let us rejoice and be about the business of the kingdom (Ps 118:24).

Lurking Constantinianism

Dionysius's calendrical invention had the effect of privileging the kingdom of God over the Empire of Rome as the driving force of history. But in the time of Dionysius, the mid-sixth century, the Roman Empire lay in ruins anyway. Rome herself, where Dionysius lived, existed only as the shell of a city. She had never fully recovered from the sack of 410. She had recently been conquered by the Byzantine Emperor Justinian who invaded Italy in the 530s. The population had dropped in proportion to its decline in prestige and prominence. Fewer than 75,000 inhabitants remained in the eternal city of Rome, and this number would go even lower in the coming years. The proud city had become a reliquary—a repository of religious relics and historical curiosities from a now-foreign past. All around, the western territories of Italy, Gaul, Britain, Germany, and Africa fragmented into pockets of local defense and vast stretches of no-man's land, the result of a process of decay that had been happening for over a hundred years.

The power vacuum wanted filling, and to many it seemed that the Christian faith and Christian leaders could fill it. Who better to assume civic authority than Christian leaders guided by Christian principles? What better vision of society than one ruled by biblical justice, one modeled on the new Jerusalem? Unfortunately, such a vision was and is a mirage, an illusion, a grand temptation, and one that has appeared in many eras under many pretexts. It goes by the name of Constantinianism.

Constantinianism refers to the settlement of Emperor Constantine (272–337) whereby the state underwent a certain degree of Christianization.[13] Constantine was the first emperor to identify himself publically as a Christian and encourage his subjects to adopt the Christian faith. From all appearances, he intended to use the Christian faith as glue that could repair the fractured Roman Empire. If the state and its inhabitants could undergo baptism in the waters of Christian morality and charity, the Empire might find its illusive unity. His dream of Christianization was never fully realized in his own lifetime, but his name is forever associated with the attempt.

The fusion of church and state proved to be more feasible in the sixth century of Dionysius than it ever was in the days of Constantine, and that made it all the more tempting. The idea of replacing old Rome with a new and Christianized version danced before the eyes of many in Dionysius's generation like glimmering pieces of silver. Christian leaders of that era had the noble but quixotic ambition of bringing the kingdom of heaven down to earth and creating a Christendom.

Whether in Roman antiquity or modern day America, the result of such ambition was and is always the same: the kingdom of heaven gets reduced to another kingdom of earth. This is Constantinianism, and it is a scourge that, from a theological point of view, is always best avoided. Whether baptizing the Empire of Rome or Christianizing the law and government of the United States of America, the kingdom of God does not benefit and flourish. Instead, it gets divided like Christ's garment into little kingdoms of gods. The year of the Lord's favor seems to be proclaimed, but the message falls short of liberty to the captives and release to the prisoners. Favor extends only to those loyal to the regime and obedient to the powers. The zealous cry out "Jesus is Lord"—not in humble submission but as a rallying cry against hated enemies.[14]

---

13. The term is credited to John Howard Yoder, *Priestly Kingdom*, 135–47.

14. This is George Lindbeck's famous example: "the crusader's battle cry '*Christus est Dominus*' . . . is false when used to authorize cleaving the skull of infidel." No matter how

And this, then, is the ultimate point of caution about Christmas. By all means, we should celebrate the birth of our Lord proudly, beautifully, and boisterously. We have reached a high-water mark in the Christian calendar and a moment for solemn reflection on the deepest mystery of our religion—the incarnation. We have much to cheer and be glad about. But not at the expense, coercion, or degradation of our non-Christian neighbors. We must avoid the Constantinian ambition to impose, conform, and regulate all. Forcibly imposed good news is not good news.

I would hope that we would also show compassion and understanding to people from other faith traditions or no faith tradition whatsoever who might take offense at the BC/AD numbering system. We shamefully betray the theological significance of the *anno Domini*—the year of the Lord's favor marked by a crown of beauty instead of ashes and the oil of joy instead of mourning (Isa 61:3)—if we use the BC/AD nomenclature as a swollen-chested gesture of vainglory meant to marginalize and exclude those outside the faith. We falsify our testimony when we come at it with an I-don't-care-who-it-offends attitude. If we use the *anno Domini*, we must do so with humility and grace, showing respectful deference to those who do not.

This admonition is not as easy to follow as it might appear. News reporters regularly churn the Christmas outrage with stories about civil liberty groups suing municipalities for displaying nativity scenes on public property. After a handful of Supreme Court decisions in the 1980s that opened the door to legal challenges, different cities have either fought to keep their Christmas displays or been forced to change them.[15] In 2014, for example, the town of Jay, Florida, chose not to erect its crèche on the lawn of city hall for the first time in forty years rather than pay $100,000 in legal fees to defend the display.[16] You might remember another story of Christmas outrage from 2005 when the mega retailer Target decided to eschew the language of "Christmas" in its marketing and signage in favor of more bland descriptors like, "Happy Holidays," "Holiday Catalogs," and "Holiday Shipping." The rumor spread that Target had forbidden employees to say

earnest the confession may be, it falsifies the essential feature of Christ's lordship—sacrificial love of one's neighbor. Lindbeck, *Nature of Doctrine*, 64.

15. *Lynch v. Donnelly* (1984) and *County of Allegheny v. ACLU* (1989). Both of these cases made application of the guidelines set out in *Lemon v. Kurtzman* (1971).

16. Kelly, "Nativity Scene Removed," *Sun* (December 14, 2014), accessed September 6, 2015, https://www.opposingviews.com/i/religion/nativity-scene-removed-florida-city-hall-after-being-deemed-illega.

"Merry Christmas." Although untrue, lathered customers wrote angry letters of protest and coalitions soon formed to ban the chain.

The latest hullabaloo: Starbucks disposable coffee cups. In November of 2015 Starbucks released its holiday cups—a simple red cup with the green Starbucks logo. The red cup represented somewhat of a divergence from previous years' holiday-themed cup designs. While these had never been religious per se, they did feature things like reindeer and tree ornaments. Certain Christian bloggers and social media personalities took the new minimalist cup as a sign of Starbucks' war on Christmas and hatred of Jesus.[17] Their response was to ask all good Christian souls who placed orders at Starbucks to request baristas to write "Merry Christmas" on their cups instead of their names.

Other Christians rolled their eyes toward the heavens—#firstworldproblems.

At Christmastime—especially at Christmastime—Christians feel an acute sense of ownership and obligation. The feeling goes much deeper than any municipal holiday decoration or commercial store policy; it is rooted in theological convictions about the essence and heart of their faith in Jesus the Christ, the Savior whose birth to a virgin is celebrated at just this time of year. These issues do not resolve themselves nicely, simply, or easily. They require faithfulness, courage, patience, and most of all, obedience to the two commandments that matter most: loving the Lord our God and our neighbor as ourselves.

Complications with the Year

Like a Christmas tour bus that has made an unexpected detour to drive by some odd light display, we have made an odd side trip to investigate the origins of the BC/AD system. But, like a good tour guide, I want to get us back on track. I would argue that the detour was relevant to our conversation about Christmas because the year of Jesus' birth is directly related to it. You will remember we began with the question, what year was Jesus born? The question cannot be answered in a clean-cut way because, as we have seen, the year itself was invented to mark the year. And this makes the following

---

17. "'Starbucks removed Christmas from their cups because they hate Jesus': Evangelists criticize Starbucks' red holiday cups," *Daily Mail* (November 8, 2015), accessed November 9, 2015, http://www.dailymail.co.uk/news/article-3309472/Evangelists-upset-Starbucks-red-holiday-cups.html.

question the more pressing: is there historical evidence to support AD 1 as the most probable year of the nativity? Or does the evidence suggest a different year?

Three different biblical clues come into play: the death of Herod the Great, the fifteenth year of Tiberius, and the census of Quirinius. Unfortunately, each clue proves as problematic as it is helpful.

First, *the death of Herod.* Matthew 2:1 and Luke 1:5 tie Jesus' birth to the reign of Herod the Great. They both indicate that Mary delivered while Herod was still alive. Scholars believe Herod died in early April 4 BC, so the birth of Jesus could not have been later than that. Herod's own death date is ascertained from two markers found in the first-century historian of Jewish antiquities, Josephus (37–94). Josephus mentions in his history of the events an eclipse just prior to Herod's death *and* the observance of the Jewish Passover just after it. The eclipse occurred in March while Passover took place in April of the year 4 BC. For these reasons, the renowned New Testament scholar Raymond Brown favors this time frame, March/April 4 BC, as the best supported and most likely window of time for Jesus' birth.[18] On the other hand, if Jesus was indeed born December 25, as tradition holds, then it must have been in the year 5 BC, a few days prior to the beginning of year 4 and a few months prior to Herod's death.

So, in this reckoning of things, Jesus seems to have been born at least four years before "the year of our Lord." How embarrassing for Dionysius Exiguus! It seems he made a mathematical error in his calculations. He should have labeled 4 BC as Year One. It is tempting to chalk his apparent error up to a simple miscalculation. We assume that he probably did the best he could with the fragmentary information at his disposal. But this excuse will not do, because Dionysius's choice of AD 1 was odd even by the standards of his sixth-century contemporaries.

Almost all other ancient authorities dated the nativity earlier than AD 1. Most dated the event to the year 3 BC. For example, Clement of Alexandria asserted that Jesus was born in the twenty-eighth year of the Emperor Augustus's reign, a year that translates to about 3 or 2 BC. Julius Africanus and Hippolytus of Rome suggested that the incarnation of the Lord occurred at the midpoint of the sixth millennium since the beginning of the world, that is, in the five-thousand-five-hundreth year of the cosmos, a

---

18. Brown, *Birth of the Messiah*, 167, 607.

date that corresponds to the second year of the one-hundred-ninety-fourth Olympiad and, interestingly enough, to the common era year of 3 BC. From Eusebius of Caesarea in the Roman east to Prosper of Aquitania in the far west, the agreed upon year of the incarnation was consistently chalked a few years before Year One.[19] Even the Gnostic *Gospel of the Infancy of the Savior* dates the nativity to about the year 4 or 3 BC. According to the text, Jesus was born in the three-hundred-ninth year of the era of Alexander, a time that corresponds to 4 or 3 BC. The collaborative agreement of all these diverse and ancient witnesses regarding the year of the nativity raise the question of how Dionysius, who was living in Rome and had access to the best information, could have miscalculated so horrendously.

The fifteenth year of Tiberius. Herod's death presents one factor, but there are two others. A second clue from the Bible regarding the year of Jesus' birth is the reign of Tiberius. Luke notes that Jesus began his ministry at the age of thirty, in the fifteenth year of Tiberius's reign (3:1, 3:23).[20] Can we determine what year that was? Caesar Augustus died in August of AD 14 and Tiberius made a smooth and immediate transition into the role of emperor following his death. Even so, should we count AD 14 as the first year of his reign or does his reign officially begin at the start of AD 15? When his tenure officially starts makes a difference because fifteen years later would take us either to the year 29 or to the year 30. The church historian Eusebius of Caesarea (260/265–339/340) informs us that the fifteenth year of Tiberius was also the fourth year of Pontius Pilate's rule as Procurator of Judaea.[21] The date range of 29 or 30 would fit well with Eusebius's information about Pilate. If Jesus underwent baptism and began his ministry in the year AD 29 or 30 at the age of thirty then, correspondingly, he must have been born about 1 BC or AD 1.

We are brought back to the calculations of Dionysius Exiguus. Perhaps we dismissed him too soon. Perhaps he did not miscalculate. Perhaps he was working off of his knowledge of the reign of Tiberius.

To summarize, we have two possible date ranges: one determined in relation to the death of Herod (approximately 5 to 4 BC) and the other in relation to the baptism of Jesus (around 1 BC or AD 1).

---

19. Mosshammer, *Easter Computus*, 325–31.

20. Hoehner, *Chronological Aspects*, 14–27.

21. Eusebius, *Historia Ecclesiastica* 1.10.1.

The census and Quirinius. Just when our discussion could not get more confused, Luke adds another detail—the imperial census carried out by Quirinius, or *Kureniou* (Κυρηνίου), as his name appears in Greek (2:2). This is the third nugget of biblical information to examine. According to Luke, the "decree went out from Caesar Augustus" (2:1). Luke suggests it was an empire-wide registration and calls it an *apographi* (ἀπογραφή). The Roman ruler Octavian, known to history as Caesar Augustus, lived from BC 63 to AD 14 and issued three major and empire-wide registrations in the years BC 28, BC 8, and AD 14, respectively. Unfortunately, none of these registrations present themselves as likely candidates for the one mentioned by Luke. It is possible that Luke had his imperial registrations mixed up, but not necessarily. Perhaps Luke did not mean that the census was empire-wide, but only that the order to perform the census came from Augustus himself. We must remember that besides these three general registrations ordered by Augustus, other regional enrollments and censuses occurred in places like Syria, Gaul, and Spain. It is possible that the edict issued "throughout all the world," the *oikoumeni* (οἰκουμένη) as Luke describes it, reflects the ongoing census process of this period.[22]

Luke himself clarifies which census of Caesar Augustus he means. He says it was the first one while Quirinius was governor of Syria. That it was the *first* and that it occurred while Quirinius was over *Syria* seem noteworthy details. They suggest that Luke considered this a memorable event and something that most of his readers would immediately recall. Josephus remembered the census on account of the Jewish people's reaction to it. They regarded it as a completely unwelcome innovation and openly revolted.[23] We need not look far to find the reason for their opposition. Imperial registration implied more than the collection of accurate population data, it meant increased taxes. It would include the inhabitant's name, age, occupation, wife, and children, and was done for the purpose of establishing military service and head tax.[24]

Modern tax programs collect from the individual a portion of his or her personal income. The Roman system, by contrast, taxed the region, not the individual. Roman-style taxation was collective, not personal. The Empire assessed regions or districts based on size and other economic factors but left it up to the town councilors—the leading men of each locality—to

22. Bock, *Luke*, 904.

23. Josephus, *Antiquities* 17.13.2, 530–31; 17.13.5, 534–37; 18.1.1, 1–9.

24. Bovon, *Luke*, 83.

diffuse the burden equitably and collect from all citizens. Ideally all inhabitants would "chip in" their fair share to the town councilors who would transfer the amount faithfully to the imperial coffers. We know from the long trail of complaints made at every level of citizenry that the system was nagged by corruption. One need only think of the scorn poured on the tax-collectors in the Gospels. Even when applied as equitably as possible, this particular system did not take into account the ups and downs of finances and fortunes. The same amount was demanded and extracted regardless of whether it had been a good year or a bad year for crops and business.

Josephus says that the dreaded tax enrollment occurred in the thirty-seventh year after Octavian's defeat of Antony at Actium in 31 BC. Thirty-seven years after 31 BC comes to AD 6. This date coincides with records that show that Quirinius served as military governor of Syria between AD 6 and 9. But, this presents a real puzzle for us. Could Jesus have been born as late as AD 6? If so, it would mean that he was born well after the death of Herod. It would also mean that he began his ministry at the tender age of twenty-four, if he began in the year 30. If, on the other hand, he began his ministry at the age of thirty, then he began at a rather late date of AD 36, and died at the even later date of AD 39. Pontius Pilate himself had already been dead for three years by that time.

For these reasons and others, the biblical scholar Emil Schürer took a bold step in 1890 and asserted that Luke was flat-out mistaken in his dating of the Quirinian census.[25] Luke erroneously believed that the census occurred about ten years earlier than it actually did. Schürer said that the Bethlehem census was simply different than the Quirinian census. It should be noted that not all commentators are convinced by Schürer's strong conclusion. Some offer other ways to reconcile the discrepancy. It is possible that Quriunius was governor twice, once from 6 to 4 BC and then again from AD 6 to 9. Another theory is that while he served as legate between Varus and Gaius Caesar between 4 and 1 BC he also held the post of military governor of Syria, and that this was when the census occurred. Or it could be the case that he merely administrated the census, but was not governor at that time. Alternatively, perhaps the confusion stems from a mistranslation. Some scholars suggest that the word *proti* (πρώτη) should not be translated as "first"—as in the "first census of Quirinius"—but as "earlier than" or "before." That is to say, maybe Luke was directing his reader's attention to a census earlier than the well-known Quirinian one of AD 6 or

---

25. Schürer, *History of the Jewish People* vol. 1, 105–43.

perhaps to a census before Quirinius's governorship altogether.[26] That is to say, there might be a couple of ways to resolve the dilemma.

What year was Jesus born? We have made a hopscotch journey through the data and your guess is as good as mine. We have seen that the Gospels and the historical record present at least three different groups of candidates: 5/4 BC is one, 1 BC/AD 1 is another, and AD 6 is a third.

Kepler's nova. And I might make mention of just one more possible candidate: 6 BC. In 1614, the famous astronomer Johannes Kepler published a book-length investigation of the date of the nativity. After observing the conjunction of Jupiter and Saturn and the concomitant appearance of a new star (a nova) that remained visible to the eye for a year, Kepler calculated that the same conjunction occurred in the month of December, 7 BC. The astronomical conjunction was followed by the appearance of a nova shortly after and must have remained visible until December of 6 BC. This he identified as the time of Christ's birth. After a lifetime of studying the geometric and harmonious movements of the stars and planets, Kepler expected to find these same rhythms at work in the most important event in the Bible.[27] Interestingly, his proposed date gained a following for some reason and held sway at the popular level for years. As proof, consider the *Encyclopedia Britannica* entry on Jesus: "born *circa* 6 BC, Judaea."[28]

In summary, the date range for the birth of Jesus falls somewhere between 6 BC at the earliest and AD 6 at the very latest. Yes, but what year exactly was Jesus born? When you get to heaven, you'll have to ask.

26. Bock, *Luke*, 909, 903–917.

27. Owen Gingerich, "Kepler's *De Vero Anno*," in Barthel and Kooten, eds., *Star of Bethlehem*, 3–16. Matthew's star has been variously identified as a nova sighted in March/April of 5 BC, or a comet (perhaps Halley's Comet) that streaked across the sky in 12 BC, or the conjunction of Venus and Jupiter in August of 3 BC and again in 2 BC. Raymond Brown surveys the theories and provides references but concludes with an important observation that is both self-evident and for that reason easily overlooked. "Matthew says that the magi saw the star (not planets, not a comet) of the King of the Jews at its rising (or in the East), and that it went before them from Jerusalem to Bethlehem and came to rest over where the child was. In recent literature I have not found an astronomical proposal that fits that literally." Brown, *Birth of the Messiah*, 612. Even those who want to find an exact astronomical occurrence to match Matthew's description fail to take Matthew's words *literally*. All are required to consider the symbolic or figurative meaning of the star, even as we try to place it physically in the sky.

28. See Mosshammer, *Easter Computus*, 323–34.

The Joyous Day

The above survey of historical data is admittedly tedious and in many respects frustrating. And if you'd known in advance how uncertain the final answer would be, you might have skipped it altogether. It shows, if nothing else, that our guesses have not advanced much beyond Dionysius Exiguus's sixth-century tabulations. Looking at the bits of historical information is like picking up pieces of an enormous jigsaw puzzle after it has been blown by a fan across the floor. We inspect each piece for a minute, turning it in our fingers only to put it down and find a new one to consider.

Let us move from the year to the actual day, about which we have even less direct information. It would be difficult to conjecture from the biblical sources even the season of the birth, let alone the exact day. Nevertheless, we are not without clues. Three perspectives should be considered in trying to pinpoint a day: first, the timing of the pregnancy; second, the witness of the early church; and third, the issue of solar timing.

Timing of the Conception

First, we should examine the biblical evidence regarding *the timing of the conception*. We start by looking for clues within the biblical text itself. As it turns out, the date of Mary's conception and delivery can be approximated from the timing of her cousin Elizabeth's pregnancy. The angel Gabriel appeared to Zechariah, husband of Elizabeth and father of John the Baptizer, on the day he was chosen by lot to enter the sanctuary of the Lord and offer incense (Luke 1:9). Zechariah belonged to the tribe of Levi, the one tribe especially selected by the Lord to serve as priests. Not restricted to any one tribal territory, the Levite priests dispersed throughout the land of Israel. Nevertheless, many chose to live near Jerusalem in order to fulfill duties in the Temple, just like Zechariah who resided at nearby Ein Karem. Lots were cast regularly to decide any number of priestly duties: preparing the altar, making the sacrifice, cleaning the ashes, burning the morning or evening incense. Yet, given the drama of the event, it would seem that he entered the Temple sanctuary on the highest and holiest day of the year, the Day of Atonement, Yom Kippur. There, beside the altar of the Lord, a radiant angel gave news of the child to be born to Elizabeth. The date reckoned for this occurrence is September 24, based on computations from the Jewish calendar in accordance with Leviticus 23 regarding the Day of Atonement.

According to Luke 1:26, Gabriel's annunciation to Mary took place in the "sixth month" of Elizabeth's pregnancy. That is, Mary conceives sixth months after Elizabeth. Luke repeats the uniqueness of the timing in verse 36. Counting six months from September 24 we arrive at March 25, the most likely date for the annunciation and conception of Mary. Nine months hence takes us to December 25, which turns out to be a surprisingly reasonable date for the birthday. Someone might object that the birth could not have occurred in midwinter because it would have been too cold for shepherds in the fields keeping watch by night (Luke 2:8). Not so. In Palestine, the months of November through February mark the rainy season, the only time of the year sheep might find fresh green grass to graze. During the other ten months of the year, animals must content themselves on dry straw. So, the suggestion that shepherds might have stayed out in the fields with their flocks in late December, at the peak of the rainy season, is not only reasonable, it is most certain.

Early Church Records

The idea that Elizabeth conceives in September and Mary in March corresponds to the traditional church calendar. Early on in its history, the church highlighted March 25 as the date for the conception of our Lord.[29] The date also marked the day on which the full-grown Jesus was thought to have suffered crucifixion. The spring equinox fell on that date, and liturgically the church remembered the creation of humankind on March 25. Honorius of Autun says that March 25 marks the day on which Adam ate from the forbidden tree. In addition, he says, John the Baptist and James were beheaded on this day.[30] Honorius observes a serendipitous symmetry to all these events. God does not commerce in random happenstance. God's providence orchestrates the tiniest details into a grand symphony of salvation. Honorius might be on to something.

And so, besides considering the timing of the conception, we must take note of *the earliest church records*. We have evidence from the second century, less than fifty years after the close of the New Testament, that Christians were remembering and celebrating the birth of the Lord. It is not true to say that the observance of the nativity was imposed on Christians

29. Augustine, *Trinity,* 4.5.9.

30. Honorius of Autun, *In annunciatione Sancta Mariae, Patrologia Latina* 172:901D–903A; Saward, *Cradle,* 320–1.

hundreds of years later by imperial decree or by a magisterial church ruling. The observance sprang up organically from the authentic devotion of ordinary believers. This in itself is important. But, besides the fact that early Christians did celebrate the incarnation of the Lord, we should make note that they did not agree upon a set date for the observance. There was no one day on which all Christians celebrated Christmas in the early church.

Churches in different regions celebrated the nativity on different days. The late second-century Egyptian instructor of Christian disciples, Clement of Alexandria, reported that some believers in his area observed the twenty-fourth or twenty-fifth day of the Egyptian month of Parmuthi (the month that corresponds to the Hebrew month of Nisan—approximately April 19 and 20), others the twenty-fifth of Pachon (approximately May 20).[31] The Basilidian Christians held to the eleventh or fifteenth of Tubi (January 6 and 10). Clement made his own computations by counting backward from the death of Emperor Commodus, the son of Marcus Aurelius. By this method he deduced a birthdate of November 18. Other Alexandrian and Egyptian Christians adopted January 4 or 5. In so doing, they replaced the Alexandrian celebration of the birth of Aion, or Time, with the birth of Christ. The regions of Nicomedia, Syria, and Caesarea celebrated Christ's birthday on Epiphany, January 6.[32]

One fascinating anonymous work called *De Pascha Computus*, written in the year 243, proposed a date of March 28. In a mind-boggling feat of mathematics, the mysterious author of *De Pascha Computus* calculated from the date of creation, the Exodus, the threefold numerology of the cross, the Greek letter *tau*, the total of the numbers represented by the letters in Jesus' name, and the date of his death—and arrived at March 28.[33] Needless to say, the author of *De Pascha Computus* did not tally the birthday from historical information, yet many Christians shared and still share his impulse toward the symbolic and the theological, even at the expense of the historic.

---

31. Clement, *Stromateis*, 1.21.

32. An added difficulty involves the interpretation of the ancient sources. When they speak of the incarnation of the Lord or the feast of the incarnation, sometimes they mean the day of his birth and sometimes they mean the annunciation to Mary and conception, two events separated by nine months. The sources are not always clear as to which meaning is intended.

33. See Roll, *Toward the Origins*, 81–82. It is not clear whether *De Pascha Computus* was calculating the birth or conception of the Lord.

Some liturgical theologians of the early church reasoned that Christ's birth should be remembered on the first day of the new year, reinforcing the symbolism of new beginnings in Christ. The advent of Christ marks the beginning of a new time, a new covenant, a new testament, and new life (2 Cor 5:17, Rev 21). The problem with celebrating Christ's birth on New Year's Day was not theological, it was practical. The Roman Senate declared January 1 the start of the new year, but other calendars such as the Egyptian, Syro-Macedonian, and the Jewish Babylonian calendars all operated differently and figured New Year's differently.[34] So, the practical question was always: what day is New Year's Day? When does the new year start?

According to researcher Susan Roll, the *Chronograph* or Philocalian Calendar is the earliest authentic document to place the birth of Jesus on December 25.[35] The production of the *Chronograph* in Rome can be dated with precision to the year 336. The *Chronograph* is a historian's treasure trove. This wide-ranging almanac contains, among other things, a Paschal table for determining the annual date of Easter, an inventory of the prefects of the city of Rome, a comprehensive listing of the bishops of Rome starting with the apostle Peter, a calendar of civic feasts and sessions of the Senate, a calendar of martyrs, illustrated depictions of the cities of Alexandria, Constantinople, Trier, and Rome, the four capitals of the realm, pictures of planets and omens associated with them, and a zodiac. The *Chronograph* is an important record of holidays, history, and timekeeping from the late classical world. But it is also important because it catches in mid-step the movement from traditional pagan culture to Christian culture. It freezes a transitional moment in time, a moment between two great epochs, the classical world of Roman antiquity and the Christian era. Both Christian bishops and Roman officials are present in it. Holy martyrs and zodiac omens of fortune sit side by side. In one document, two world views, the traditional Roman and the new Christian, are preserved for our consideration.

The *Chronograph* does not represent the efforts of a single hand. In actuality, it is a rolling collection of calendars, catalogs, and informational charts. It's a compilation. More than one entry in the *Chronograph* identifies December 25 as Jesus' birthday.[36] And we should remember that although

34. Mosshammer, *Easter Computus*, 34–38.

35. The *Chronograph* is also known as the Philocalian Martyrology, the Catalogus Bucherianus, the Catalogus Cuspiniani, or the Calendar of Furius Dionysius Philocalus. Roll, *Toward the Origins*, 83–86.

36. Tucked away in the chronological registry of consuls, we find this note: "Christ is born during the consulate of C. Caesar Augustus and L. Aemilianus Paulus on 25

the *Chronograph* provides the first record of December 25, the custom of venerating the Lord's birth on that day was most likely established well before its publication. That is to say, December 25 didn't originate with the *Chronograph*. It must have counted as common knowledge, at least in Rome, to warrant its inclusion in the *Chronograph*. Soon after this time, we find other church fathers such as John Chrysostom, Augustine, Jerome, and Leo confirming the twenty-fifth as the traditional date of celebration. Other contenders faded away quickly and December 25 became the most widely recognized date for the birth of the Christ.

Birthday of the Invincible Sun

In addition to the biblical clues and the witness of the early church, there is a third consideration: *solar awareness*. December 25 marked the traditional winter solstice in the Julian calendar, the shortest day of the year, after which the days would progressively grow longer and the nights shorter. Greeks and Romans marked the season with midwinter festivals, the Lenaea and Saturnalia respectively. From a sociological perspective, it is not surprising that Christians would also find a way to mark the season.

One intriguing theory suggests that the choice of December 25 represented either an accommodation of or a challenge to the pagan "Birthday of the Invincible Sun," *sol invictus*. Possibly, Christians chose the twenty-fifth so that they might continue to enjoy pagan festivals under the guise of Christian worship. Read a different way, Christians targeted the date in order to expunge and replace the pagan celebration with a Christian one.[37]

December, a Friday, the 15th day of the new moon." Roll, *Toward the Origins*, 84.

37. This theory is not a new one. The late fourth century Scriptor Syrus conjectured that

> It was a custom of the pagans to celebrate on the same 25 December the birthday of the Sun, at which they kindled lights in token of festivity. In these solemnities and revelries the Christians also took part. Accordingly when the doctors of the Church perceived that Christians had a leaning to this festival, they took counsel and resolved that the true Nativity should be solemnized on that day.

Quoted in Hutton, *Stations of the Sun*, 1. Scriptor Syrus's easy conclusion is oversimplified and unsupported. Maximus of Turin came to a nearly opposite conclusion, namely that "the doctors of the Church" imposed Christmas on December 25 as a challenge to paganism and a thrust against the festival of the sun.

The end result was the same. Invincible Sun no longer owned the day—Jesus of Bethlehem did.

The convenience of this theory should not distract from its many historical problems. The Invincible Sun did not represent an old and powerful deity that the Christians needed to accommodate; he was a newcomer to the pantheon of gods. Aurelian, the emperor who lived from 214 to 275, introduced this new deity to the Romans when he claimed the god had revealed his favor to Rome before the battle of Emesa. Constantius followed Aurelian in the veneration of the sun. But it was his son, Constantine, who made it popular. The Unconquered Sun appeared on Constantinian coinage, and in other artistic representations featuring Constantine, including a statue of Apollo made in the likeness of Constantine in which Constantine wears a radiant crown of sun.

Constantine popularized the image of the sun, but he did so within a Christian context. He had good reason to associate solar imagery with Christian worship of Jesus Christ. Indeed, a long-standing tradition of using solar imagery in Christian worship existed prior to Constantine. Constantine could point to the fact that Christians gather for worship on "the day named after the sun."[38] Malachi 4:2 spoke of the "sun of righteousness" that would rise with healing in its rays. Many Christians applied Malachi's image to Jesus Christ. And furthermore, the visions of Christ reported by Paul in Acts 26 and John of Patmos in Revelation 1 describe him as brighter than the sun. Solar images appear on a couple of third-century catacomb frescos outside Rome and on a sculpture of Jonah understood as a symbol of resurrection. They also found their way into the liturgical practices and symbolism of many churches. The fourth-century Cyril of Jerusalem instructed new Christians to face east toward the rising sun to pray. And for Lactantius, a contemporary of Constantine, "the east is attached to God because he is the source of light and the illuminator of the world and he makes us rise toward eternal life."[39] The theological significance of the sun for Christian thinkers is boundless: it can be interpreted as a sign of divine illumination, bodily resurrection, and the source of all life.

We should not be scandalized to find elements of Christian worship and symbolism connected with natural phenomena. Christian worship of Jesus was not sun worship in disguise. Sun worship was not somehow converted and turned into Christian orthodoxy. Rather, the cycles of nature

---

38. Justin, *Apologia* 1 67.3–5.

39. Lactantius, *Divine Institutes* 2.9.5; Potter, *Constantine the Emperor*, 159.

supplied early Christians (and us!) with the pallet of God's grandeur. The texture of the natural world transmits the glory of nature's Maker. There is biblical precedent for adapting seasonal feasts to Christian contexts. The Feast of Tabernacles, for example, originated as a feast of reaping, as Leviticus 23:39 itself recognizes.[40] We people of the earth try to understand our unimaginable God through the things of the earth.

And so, we should not be surprised that our Christian ancestors found theological significance in the darkest day of the year. We should be surprised if they did not. God's dominion extends over nature as well as human affairs. The puritanical desire to sponge away associations with the seasonal cycles for fear of pagan contamination is misguided at best, and atheistic at worst. It is atheistic in the sense that it seeks to disassociate God with all things earthly so as to protect God's holiness, but inadvertently disassociates God with us humans—who are the earthiest of all. How could Christians not notice the annual day of short light and long night? And how could they not reflect on it and on its Creator?

Whether conscious or unconscious, the pairing of the birthday of the Lord with the Unconquered Sun and with the winter solstice made for fertile theological reflection. Even if the sun had not been remembered in late December by the Romans, there still would have been a strong theological rationale to commemorate Christ's advent during the darkest time of the year. On a day short and cold the arrival of God's child warms the heart. The birth of Christ welcomes new light. The light will only grow in strength as the days progress and steadily lengthen. The long night is over, the dawn of new day has come.[41]

Some readers will feel a pinch of exasperation at this point in the narrative. Some will want to throw up hands and say, "Who knows! Who cares! What difference does the year or day make?" Such an attitude will not do. We must not overlook the historical minutiae because those details help us understand that in every way God has identified with our condition. The majestic King of kings did not just pluck up one lucky individual to do his bidding nor did the eternal Word of God manifest one sunny afternoon from heaven fully dressed and ready for business. No, the God of the

---

40. Daniélou, *Bible and the Liturgy*, 334.

41. The solar symbolism only works in the northern hemisphere, in Europe, China, Japan, and North America. South of the equator, it should be remembered, in Australia, New Zealand, southern Asia, India, Africa, and Latin America, where the seasons are inversed, the symbolism is also inverted.

universe came as all of us come—through the birth canal (1 Cor 11:12). Part of human history is the gritty tedium of figuring out dates.

Even so, we must now turn from the timing of the event to its location.

The Rule of Bedlam

In the blood-drained year of 1865, an Episcopal priest named Phillips Brooks had a unique opportunity to make pilgrimage to the Holy Land. Moved by his experience of Bethlehem, he returned to his disunited states of America and the tangles of civil war to write his much-beloved hymn, "O Little Town of Bethlehem." From the deep and dreamless sky where the silent stars go by to the dark streets of hopes and fears, the Reverend Brooks gave witness to the desperate desire of the human condition for that everlasting Light from above to descend to us, cast out all sin and enter in.[1]

In the nonstop department-store blitz of holiday tunes, it's easy to forget about Brooks's gentle hymn. After a while, all holiday songs overlap, intermingle, and interbreed until they create a single jingling bell of noise. Even so, the carol endures. Its melody lilts with quiet restraint; its somber words whisper a deep hope to those who sing it. Is it a song of sadness or of joy? Is the sky dreamless and the stars silent because of some great sickness or because of some great anticipation? Are the streets dark in spite of the light? Or is the light dispelling the last remaining blots of darkness? One wonders if both hope and fear can meet and if one will win out over the other. His lyrics capture the conflicted meanings of Bethlehem itself, a town less than ten miles south of Jerusalem off Highway 60 in the Palestinian West Bank. Having existed for over 3,000 years, the town can trace its origins to the primitive Canaanites who once bore their young and buried their dead there. Indeed, some believe the name of the place derives from the name of the Canaanite god, Lachama.[2]

1. Mulder and Roberts, *28 Carols to Sing*, 116–21.
2. The Canaanite *lachama*, the Chaldean *lakhmu*, and the Hebrew *leḥem* are all

In an unexpected turn of history, this sleepy prehistoric town came to hold sway over the imagination of the biblical narrative. Rachel, Jacob's beloved wife, died there. Her shrine can be visited today. The stories of Naomi and Ruth and the great King David are tethered to it as well. Matthew 2:6 presents the looming puzzle of the place in a citation of Micah 5:2:

> And you, Bethlehem, in the land of Judah,
>
> are by no means least among the rules of Judah;
>
> for from you shall come a ruler
>
> who is to shepherd my people Israel.[3]

Matthew places these words upon the lips of "the chief priests and scribes of the people" in answer to King Herod's question: "Where is the child who has been born king of the Jews?" (Matt 2:2–4). It was not really Herod's question. The wise men asked it. And just as the question did not originate with King Herod, so the answer given by the priests and scribes did not originate with them but with the Hebrew prophet Micah. In this way, the scribes smartly deflected the question by referring it to the scrolls. When the wise men asked Herod about the newborn king, Herod asked his religious scribes, who turned attention from themselves to the ancient scroll of Micah. And so, we have a secondhand answer for a secondhand question.

In the verse quoted above from Matthew, and before that, from Micah, Bethlehem is lauded for giving Israel her ruler and shepherd. And like that, this beautiful verse became forever joined to the wonder of Christmas. Yet, we should take a moment to consider the original context of the verse. That is, how does this verse fit with the surrounding verses in Micah 5 and how does it figure into Micah's overall message?

---

interconnected terms and relate to fertility, grain, and bread. It is very possible that grain fertility was personified as a sacred deity and that the town was originally named for the deity, *Beit Lachama*, "House of Lachama," and later morphed into "House of Bread," *Bethlehem*. George, *Rod in the Old Testament*, 77.

3. The careful reader might note a slight textual variation between Matthew's Greek quotation and Micah's own wording. The difference does not affect the sense of the verse. Micah 5:2 reads:

> But you, O Bethlehem of Ephrathah,
> who are one of the little clans of Judah,
> from you shall come forth for me
> one who is to rule Israel.

Micah 5:1, the verse just prior to the one we have been considering, sounds nothing like what we might expect. It rings a clanging and cacophonous cry of desperation:

> Now you are walled around with a wall;
>
> siege is laid against us;
>
> with a rod they strike the ruler of Israel
>
> upon the cheek.

Micah speaks of a siege that walls in the inhabitants with suffocating pressure. He speaks of a rod that remorselessly assaults the very authorities of Israel. He speaks of suffering and sorrow. He speaks of pain and loss. Would the Lord allow such humiliation and depredation? And, how does this context affect our understanding of the blessed incarnation of God's Son?

Hopes and Fears

From March to April 2002, Israeli military forces carried out "Operation Defensive Shield" in the West Bank, performing systematic sweeps in search of terrorist suspects, anti-Israeli agitators, and guns. As part of this large-scale operation to root out militants and "stop the terror," Bethlehem was invaded on April 1, 2002. After an initial air strike, Israeli tanks surrounded the city and entered the following day. Approximately 200 Palestinians fled the advancing Israeli forces. At first they ran toward the Umar, Bethlehem's local Muslim mosque, but it was bombed. So they turned into the Church of the Nativity across the street.[4]

From the outside, the Church of the Nativity blends in with the rest of the sun-bleached and sand-blasted buildings in the city. Despite its unassuming appearance, it remains one of the oldest continuously operating churches in the world. It dates back to the second century. The church, built on the site traditionally identified as the place of Jesus' birth, a little cave inlet, is now administered jointly by Greek Orthodox, Roman Catholic, and Armenian Apostolic authorities. All three traditions maintain monastic communities on the site. In this place of Jesus' birth we see a model of interdenominational relationship, three different Christian traditions,

---

4. "Timeline: Bethlehem Siege," *BBC News,* May 10, 2002, http://news.bbc.co.uk/2/hi/middle_east/1950331.stm, accessed March 4, 2015.

Greek, Roman, and Armenian, living side by side, working and worshiping together.

The desperate Palestinians shot down the door of the Church of the Nativity with machine guns and rushed inside for cover. Israeli forces immediately surrounded the church and prepared for a standoff. During the thirty-nine–day siege, the Palestinians took a candelabrum and some icons and other objects that looked like gold. But, they did no harm to the monks. In fact, the Christian monks shared with the Palestinians what food they had—a brave act of hospitality in the midst of danger and confusion. They huddled together to avoid being shot. A church bell ringer and nine Palestinians were killed by sniper fire and many more wounded during the standoff. After more than a month of tension, worldwide media coverage, the involvement of the Vatican and the United States government—President Bush had instructed Israel to back down because the Israelis had entered Bethlehem without just cause to do so—the siege ended. Eventually, the 200 Palestinians made an agreement for surrender and deportation, and exited the church without gunfire. A bloodbath was averted.

So much converged upon this scene at one time. Hopes and fears met in the birth place of the Savior that became the dramatic stage for a twenty-first–century showdown, complete with tanks and grenades and automatic weapons. A Christian church became the refuge for Muslim Palestinians fleeing from a Jewish army. Jews, Muslims, and Christians got caught in a complicated web of violence and fear on the spot where the Son of God was born as an infant to a frightened, newlywed couple. In view of this event and other Middle Eastern calamities, we are tempted to despair. Was the birth of a son so long ago in this little town all for nothing? Will Christ's message of peace and forgiveness finally be drowned out by gunfire, car bombs, and screaming mothers? Does it all boil down to survival of the fittest, might makes right, salvation by the sword? Can the everlasting light of Christ be found, and will it be enough?

There is hope, even in this grim scene. The Israelite army did not rush the church in an all-out assault; the Palestinians did not charge out with guns blazing. Eventually they laid down their weapons. Diplomacy worked. The Christian monks inside did not choose sides, did not call for a violent ending, but continued their prayers and services and Bible readings.

God Gave Them Up

Returning to Micah 5:1 we find that Micah foresaw a day when Jerusalem would be surrounded by enemies, besieged and reduced to rubble. Within one hundred years of the prophet's lifetime, in fact, his prophecy came true. It was bound to happen. Micah lived in a violent age, an age of uncertainty and turmoil. Jesus was also born into a politically unstable environment, a moment of national crisis, one not unlike the situation of Micah 5 and not unlike the situation in the Middle East today, where complex webs of power negotiate for land and control, sometimes with treaties and sometimes with tanks.

And so Micah predicted the Lord "shall give them up" (Mic 5:3). At first glance, this phrase lacks the sound and the fury needed to grab our attention. *God gave them up.* It is an understatement in the extreme. But if we think about it, few phrases in all of Scripture are as bone-rattling as this one: *God gave them up.* To what? To clawing and scratching, panicking and grabbing, sieging, and surviving. The same phrase, "give up" or "hand over," is repeated at the climactic moment of the Gospel story. Jesus is given up to Pilate, handed over for scourging and finally given up for crucifixion (Mark 15:15; Matt 27:26; Luke 23:25; John 19:16). The Apostle Paul, in the course of describing God's wrath and response to sin, repeats the phrase three times in Romans 1—"God gave them over" (Rom 1:24, 26, 28). Paul can conceive of no greater curse than for God to give up, turn his back, and leave us to our own devices.

Someone might object that being left alone is an easier punishment than the flames of hellfire. Isn't abandonment more bearable than constant torment? Indeed, divine abandonment might even come with a human liberty of sorts—abandoned and forgotten we are free from God's eye, free from legal expectations and religious requirements. Only, it's not the liberty we think we want. It is not freedom to flourish and create and love. It is the freedom of the untethered astronaut—helpless and adrift in space. If we so choose, Micah the prophet reminds us, God allows us to go our own way and get what we want. But this does not make for real freedom; this is its own punishment. This kind of wrath is not nearly as conventional and predicable as a lightning bolt flung from the sky. It is something much worse. It is something of our own making.[5] We devise and design our own

---

5. Saint Augustine of Hippo emphasized that hell is closer to a state of being than a location of residence. Augustine, *De Genesi ad litteram* 12.62, *Patrologia Latina* 34, 480. See Balthasar, *Dare We Hope*, 127. Balthasar quotes Augustine as saying, "There is, then,

insane asylum, our own Bedlam. True divine wrath means nothing more or less than God giving up and washing his hands of us. And that, in the end, makes for a cold and lonely place.

Micah assures us, praise be to God, that the time of abandonment does not go on forever. It lasts "until the time when she who is in labor has brought forth" (Mic 5:3), a phrase that Matthew and the other New Testament Gospel writers understood as prophecy of the birth of Jesus. From Bethlehem came King David, and now from Bethlehem comes another son of David, Immanuel, God with us, the right hand of God's salvation. From the weakest and most insignificant town comes the hero of the story. "His greatness will reach to the ends of the earth. And he will be their peace" (Mic 5:4–5, NIV). Silently, as Phillip Brooks's carol understands, the child from heaven entered the world as a wondrous gift.

Untrain for War

Consider this random act of holiday violence: on Tuesday, December 11, 2012, a man wearing a ski mask entered a busy shopping mall in Portland, Oregon, where children had gathered to see Santa Claus and parents checked items off wish lists. He pulled out a rifle and sprayed bullets across the food court, killing three individuals.

As reporters covered the reaction to this holiday horror, they were interrupted later in the week by a twenty-year-old gunman who entered Sandy Hook Elementary School in Newtown, Connecticut, on Friday, December 14, shot and killed twenty kindergarten children, six adults including teachers and administrators, the school principal, and finally, himself.

This is the world we live in.

What do we do with these indigestible acts of inhumanity? Mostly, we feel shock, disgust, and dismay. "I've never seen anything like this happen. I've never even heard of anything like this happening." So said Scott Nord, the family lawyer involved in a 2008 Los Angeles case in which a disgruntled ex-husband dressed as Santa Claus, knocked on the door of his former in-laws, and then opened fire, killing nine inside.[6] Horrific deeds of violence sound to some citizens like a clarion call to arms. The bile of righteous indignation rises up and demands blood. All the more reason,

---

definitely a real hell, but I take it to affect the imagination, not the body." *De Genesi ad litteram*, 12.61, *Patrologia Latina* 34, 481.

6. "Santa Massacre Leaves 16 Orphans," *The Australian*, December 29, 2008.

some say, to pack pistols and prepare for self-defense. You shoot at me and I shoot back. Violence must be met with violence in this stand-your-ground culture.

What should be the response of a Christ-follower? "Must the sword devour forever? Don't you realize that this will end in bitterness?" (2 Sam 2:26–7). Is death by the sword the only way?

The world has plenty of examples of rough justice. The world has more than enough models of thick-skinned toughness, of hard men who arm themselves against predators and take vengeance on behalf of innocent victims. What the world needs now are some models of peace. The people of God are not called to behave like other nations. Christians do not live by the rules of revenge and power. The task of the church is to be the peace of Christ. Christians, those who follow the one born in the manger so long ago, must set the example of how to beat swords into plowshares and spears into pruning hooks, how to lay down weapons, how to untrain for war. And yet we do not do this just to set an example. Even if no one follows our example, we are still called and commanded to live peaceably, to practice reconciliation, to forgive, and to extend fellowship to all people in God's new kingdom.

In the 2002 standoff at the Church of the Nativity in Bethlehem, the arms of hostile Israelis and Palestinians met, but amazingly did not flare into a bloody end. Peace made its stand in no small part because of the silent presence of the Christians inside the humble Church of the Nativity. Christians can do more than excuse themselves from the conflicts of the world. The church can do more than turn a blind eye to injustice, murder, and oppression. The world is a violent place. We must acknowledge this fact. But we can also do more.

The world says to claim what's yours and defend it to the death. Christ says to lay down what's yours for the love of your neighbor, to astound your fellow human beings with generosity, to give grace instead of insult, to respond to hatred with kindness. It is our job to offer the world a different way so that the prophecies of Micah 4:3–5 may come true, "they shall live secure." God's plan has always been one of peace, hope, reconciliation, and we, as the children of God, have been commissioned to work toward those goals, as idealistic and, frankly, crazy as they sound.

The priests and clergy at Bethlehem's Church of the Nativity could not force the Palestinians to surrender, nor could they force the Israelis to back down. But neither would they flee the church and abandon the scene. One priest declared, "Why would we leave? We are custodians of this house." Their courage in the face of danger and their presence in the midst of death become for us a symbol of hope and a continual reminder of the alternative: peace. We live in a world burdened and broken by violence. We might be sorely tempted to abandon it to its own devices. We could, couldn't we, withdraw from public life into little enclaves of Christian communities? But why would we leave? We are custodians of this house.

Custodians of the House

The word *Bethlehem* means "house of bread," or more prosaically, "the granary." The modern Arabic name for the town, Bayt Lachm, retains that meaning. It is a name that lends itself easily to symbolic interpretation. For Christians the symbolism begins with the observation of John 6:41 that Christ is the bread of the world.[7] Just as Bethlehem marks the birthplace of the Bread of the world so the ongoing task of the new Bethlehem, the church, is to feed this saving Bread to all who are hungry and in need. The church, as the new house of bread, becomes the "perpetual Bethlehem."[8] Symbolically then, the people of God labor as bakers sifting flour, kneading dough, checking ovens, slicing, buttering, and distributing the sustenance of life. "The poor will eat and be satisfied"; "He has filled the hungry with good things" (Ps 22:26; Ps 107:9; and also Luke 1:53). The significance stretches past the symbolic to the sacramental. In the regular celebration of the communion meal, actual bread and drink are blessed and consumed, and it is for this reason that, sacramentally speaking, the church proves to be the house of bread.[9] The sacrament is one of sacrifice and praise, but it is also one of forgiveness. If bread signifies Christ's broken body, the nourishment of Christ is signified by forgiveness.

"Sacramental" implies "communal." If reconciliation constitutes a sacrament, it constitutes a communion, that is, a communal event, not an individual choice. From top to bottom, American society accentuates individuality—individual rights, opinions, and desires. We are taught that each individual should make up his or her own mind, plot his or her own course in life, and be original. We are conditioned to make our own way and do

---

7. The symbolism between the two has not been overlooked by theologians and preachers. Aquinas, *Summa Theologiae* 3a, q. 35, a. 7.

8. Ephrem, *Hymnen de Nativitate* 25.6, in *Hymns,* 200.

9. Aquinas, *Summa Theologiae* 3a, q. 35, a. 7.

what we want. When it comes to forgiveness, the same ethos applies. Forgiveness is conceived as an individual decision and duty: each person must decide for him or herself how to forgive and move on. But, in the Christian community, forgiveness and reconciliation count as sacraments, and the nature of sacrament is necessarily communal.[10] Forgiveness is not left to the discretion of the individual. It comes in the form of expected obedience to the rule of Christ and a result of participation in the collective sacrament of the church—the mystery of *koinonia*, fellowship, and friendship.

I remember watching *It's a Wonderful Life* as a kid. When it ended I thought, *Mr. Potter never got his up n' comings*. You will remember that in the Frank Capra black-and-white classic, Uncle Billy loses $8,000 on his way to making a deposit at the bank on Christmas Eve. Mr. Potter (Lionel Barrymore) finds the money but tucks it away. George Bailey (Jimmy Stewart) realizes that he will be held legally responsible for the missing deposit and nearly throws himself off a bridge in despair. Ultimately the townsfolk of Bedford Falls along with George Bailey's friends and associates pitch in to save the day and make up the missing money. The film ends without Mr. Potter getting caught, exposed, and punished. This bothered me as a youngster. As an adult, I now think the film ends brilliantly because it allows for any number of applications. In many ways the film is a parable of the kingdom of heaven. We do not get the satisfaction of seeing the wicked punished and arguably this is as it should be. The kingdom of heaven is not about vengeance on the wicked, it is about the community of the faithful coming together to encourage, support, and carry one another.

In an alternate and imaginative Quentin Tarantino version, whose title might be something like *George Bailey's Revenge*, George might track the missing money back to Mr. Potter and torture the truth out of him. But this is not what actually happens. The revenge plot, which we have all seen played out on the big screen, is the tale of a lonesome and obsessed man with nothing left to lose and no one left to whom he might turn. *It's a Wonderful Life* is a tale about the value of community, about friends you can count on in the most dire moments of life. The community of Bedford Falls saves George Bailey from losing his business and going to jail. And the church, through the collective practice of forgiveness, saves us from the lonely power of hate and retribution.

10. Aquinas, *Summa Theologiae* 3, q. 65, a. 4; Luijten, *Sacramental Forgiveness*, 142–43.

When it comes down to it, the Christian proclamation is nothing more or less than forgiveness. To the question "forgiveness of what?," the answer is "sin"—but that does not mean Christians believe in sin. Sin is absurd. It is *the* absurd. It is what goes wrong and there is never a good reason for it. To admit *belief in sin* suggests a reasonable, sensible, and possibly even good reason for it. Christians believe in God, almighty Maker of heaven and earth, in Jesus Christ his Son, and in the forgiveness offered through the cross and the empty tomb. And yet, for all the world, why shouldn't we believe in sin? We have much more evidence of it than of forgiveness. The cable news channels provide new examples of sin, crime, corruption, pride, and inhumanity every day on their never-ending twenty-four–hour rotation of reporting and commentary. Of all the theological doctrines of the Christian church, the "doctrine of sin" might be the only one we have tangible, universal proof of; in a world that often doubts the existence of God, no one doubts the existence of sin.

Although sin and selfishness are surely more evident and demonstrable, the invisible but eternal force of forgiveness is more decisive. The travails and tragedies of this world will soon fade away; God's work of reconciliation will last forever. Beneath the angry scar of sin one can see a deeper and older scar—the wound of healing love, the wound of peace.

Because God sent his only-begotten Son into the world on that cold night in Bethlehem, Christians believe that every person is redeemable and that no person puts him or herself beyond redemption. More than that, we believe that every person has been redeemed . . . already . . . 2,000 years ago when the baby boy who had grown up laid down his life on a hill outside of Jerusalem. The question has nothing to do with whether or not a person *can* be forgiven. That question has already been answered in Christ: *Yes.* The good news of Jesus Christ is the reality of forgiveness. The real question is whether or not a person will accept the free gift of forgiveness that is being extended to him or her. The gift has been purchased, paid for, wrapped, and placed under the tree with a name tag on it, but each individual has a decision to make: whether to pick it up and open it or to walk away and leave it untouched.

One Night in Missoula

In November of 2006 three youths broke into South Hills Evangelical Church, located in Missoula, Montana. The young men began their evening by cutting the locks off two trailers outside the church. Not satisfied with what they found in the trailers, they turned their attention to the main church building. The three young men broke into and roved about, spreading giddy havoc as they went. They sprayed fire extinguishers in the church gym, smashed some electronic equipment, and unloaded a vending machine in the teen center. They wandered aimlessly through the dark hallways. Meanwhile, outside a night security guard found the unattended car in the back alley. He also discovered the locks that had been cut off the trailers. He called a church trustee to come and put on new locks, not realizing that the burglars were still in the building.

When the church trustee arrived, he told the guard to remain with the vehicle in the back alley while he went inside to get two new locks. Stepping into the church office he sensed something out of place. Lights were on in the sanctuary. The trustee paused and listened. The sound of scuffling told him all he needed to know. The intruders were nearby. He called 911. The three youths made a mad dash for the side door. The night guard caught two at the getaway car while police nabbed the third as he ran down the street.

The three young men were taken to jail, booked, charged, and prosecuted. The next Sunday South Hills Evangelical's pastor, Jason Reimer, talked from the pulpit about the dramatic events of that night, the burglary and vandalism. He concluded by saying, "that's just stuff. All of that can be replaced. It's their souls that we care about." Pastor Reimer told his congregation that he wanted part of their sentences to include community service in the form of attendance at church for a year of Sundays in the front row. Perhaps it was only an offhanded remark at first, but as he continued to talk he began to realize with particular clarity that the congregation had been presented an opportunity in the form of a burglary.

What might the church want to say to these three young men? Rarely does a church have a chance to ask this question. Church facilities are hit more often than one might think with vandalism, burglary, and invasion after hours. Church buildings contain pricey electronics and sit empty for much of the week. They make for easy targets. I can testify from personal experience. All the churches I have served were at some point burglarized. I've had personal items stolen from church. Seldom are the perpetrators caught.

The congregants of South Hills Evangelical Church found themselves in a unique position. The criminals had been apprehended. The church could confront them, look them in the face . . . and say what? Some members of the church insisted that they be prosecuted to the fullest extent of the law. They should be shamed and barred from the property. Vandalism and thievery are bad enough, but when committed against a church they are even more shameful. These hooligans desecrated a sacred space; they defiled holy ground. Pastor Reimer chose not to take that view. Instead, he saw a chance to practice something taught to children in Sunday school but perhaps forgotten by the adults. The congregation sat in silence on that Sunday morning and watched as an idea began to form in his mind. "I want to do something radical," Pastor Reimer said. "I want to collect donations and give love baskets to the thieves and their families. If they wanted to steal an iPod, let's give them an iPod!" He paused, then added with a grin, "Now, don't go telling other thieves around town that we're doing this."[11]

To everyone's amazement, donations came pouring into the church. Part of the success may have been the timing. Christmas was approaching and people gave gift cards, cash, electronics, groceries, notes of encouragement and prayer. The pastor's words of caution to his congregation not to blab about the gifts had not been heeded because within a week everyone in Missoula knew about the generous love baskets. The story was printed in the local newspaper and then picked up by several national papers. Soon enough, Pastor Reimer was giving live interviews to Fox News, CNN, and the BBC.

In a world where the religion called Christianity has grown old and familiar, a genuine act of Christian charity can still surprise. And yet it surprises precisely because, at the risk of being taken advantage of or being labeled "soft" on crime, South Hills Evangelical Church witnessed to the fact that reconciliation trumps justice. The maintenance of justice is critical, to be sure, but not final. Justice is important, but it's not the highest Christian value. The highest Christian value is reconciliation, with its twin tasks of forgiveness and love. Justice can even the score, but the love and forgiveness required for reconciliation have the power to put things right.

As delightful as this story is from Missoula, Montana, it invites a serious objection, one which the pastor winked at when he said, "Now, don't go telling other thieves around town that we're doing this." Someone might object: *Christians must be completely naïve and sadly idealistic. You don't reward criminals for their bad behavior. If everyone did that, society would*

11. Jason Reimer, quoted by Jordan Green, "Four Thieves," *Burnside Writers Collective*, September 17, 2007, accessed at burnsidewriters.com on January 5, 2008.

*break down into anarchy. The only way to deter crime is to punish criminals,
and to punish them severely.*

And of course, the critic is right. Forgiveness involves risk—the risk
of being taken advantage of, the risk of being duped, the risk of failure. It
is without a doubt naïve, idealistic, and unrealistic. But the risk is precisely
what distinguishes a Christian ethic from any other. Christians are not
kinder or nicer or more prone to tell the truth than other people. Christians get divorced like other people; they break the laws like other people;
for the most part they talk and walk and dress like other people. If there is
anything distinct or unique about a Christian ethic it is the commitment,
no, the binding command to forgive.

We forgive because we are convinced of the absurd notion that the
God of the universe has extended forgiveness to us.

To forgive the way that the South Hills Evangelical Church did takes
the kind of creativity and imagination that can only issue from a full-scale
trust in the God who has entrusted us with the ministry of reconciliation
(2 Cor 5:18–21). It will not come naturally or easily. It must proceed from
the Holy Spirit. If contemporary Christian ethics has failed, its failure is one
of imagination. If it has succeeded, its success is its ability to imagine bold
acts of forgiveness. Do we have the Spirit-filled imagination to see ourselves
forgiving not once or twice, but seventy-seven times? The ministry of reconciliation means we never write off anyone because God does not write off
anyone. No one is irredeemable, no one is beyond forgiveness. Nothing we
do puts us beyond the reach of God's love. God does not need reminding
of that fact, but those of us called to announce and administer forgiveness
often do.

It is not the case that Christianity disregards crime, sin, selfishness,
and greed, so as to allow the individual to go on sinning all the more (Rom
6:15, 6:1). If anything, Christianity takes these things more seriously than
one might expect. Any breach is a fatal one; any sin is a sin unto death.
No trivial peccadillos or petty crimes slip through the keyhole of divine
justice. All sins are judged equally with the result that all have sinned and
fall short of the glory of God. The eternal glory of the Almighty allows no
unrighteousness, admits no crime, and relaxes no law. The crime must not
be excused.[12]

With this in mind we can now see that we fall into a sensible but downright unchristian trap when we meet a friend's honest "I'm sorry" with the

---

12. Chesterton, *Orthodoxy*, 97.

shrug of the shoulders and an offhanded response: "Don't worry about it. No big deal." We do wrong when we waive off an apology as unnecessary. Such a gesture dresses itself as big-hearted magnanimity but underneath one finds a parsimonious and miserly attitude toward forgiveness. The implicit logic of waiving off an apology is this: if some injuries are too small to need forgiveness then it must be the case that others are too big to receive it. If we are habituated not to forgive little sins because they are not worth trifling over, then it will be all the harder for us to forgive big ones because, so it seems, they will be more costly than any forgiveness can afford.

Forgiveness is not a form of forgetfulness. To forgive is not to forget. Forgiveness opposes forgetfulness. If something needs forgiving, it needs it precisely because it cannot be forgotten. Christian forgiveness means reconciling, making amends, building peace, bridging the gap. For this reason, when we tell a victim that he or she has two choices when dealing with hurt—either seek justice or forget about it—we speak an untruth. These two options represent a false dilemma.

I admit that sometimes it *does* seem that the person who has suffered an offense must either demand payback or let the offense go. Under the pretense of politeness this second choice often gets equated with Christian forgiveness: *forgive and forget; don't let little things get to you; be the bigger person; don't worry about it; sticks and stones will break your bones but words will never hurt you.* Whatever else this advice might be, it is not Christian.

The aim of Christian forgiveness is not to erase the offense and pretend that it didn't occur; it aims to heal, mend, and repair the relationship between offender and offended. In this sense, Christian forgiveness has a different objective than the American judicial system. The mandate of the judicial system treats every individual fairly and equally. Most importantly, it holds each citizen accountable to the law, subject to the law's protections and punishments. By contrast, Christian forgiveness does not hope to ensure justice and fairness for all parties. It intends to go one step further to the restoration of relationship. Christian forgiveness aims to put relationships right, make friends of enemies, and allow people to recognize in the face of the other a brother and a sister.

Put to the Test

A month before the Missoula, Montana break-in, a much more serious break-in occurred in Nickel Mines, Pennsylvania when Charles Carl

Roberts IV, a local milk truck driver, entered a one-room schoolhouse in Amish country. Roberts bound and shot ten girls, five of whom died, before killing himself. The story was especially jarring and tragic because it happened in such a peaceful place—in a schoolhouse, in rural Pennsylvania, in Amish country. As the news cameras and media swarmed Nickel Mines to cover the story, they found something unexpected and amazing underneath the horror. They found that the Amish, as a community, refused to hate Roberts; they chose instead to forgive. One grandfather was overheard saying to his grandsons, "We must not think evil of this man."[13]

The Amish chose not to surrender to feelings of bitter anger at their own loss but to follow the command of Christ to love our enemies. They did this not because they are somehow superior to other American citizens or because their human nature is any different than ours. The Amish are near cousins of the Baptists, descendants of the sixteenth-century Reformation, and with their Reformation heritage comes a special love for the Lord's Prayer. They recite it at every worship service, every wedding and every funeral. Amish schoolhouses begin their days with the Lord's Prayer. It is the prayer that most Amish pray silently before and after meals, and the prayer that fathers say over their children as they lay them down.

At the heart of that prayer is this insistence that receiving forgiveness is connected and dependent upon giving forgiveness: "and forgive us our trespasses as we forgive those who trespass against us" (Matt 6:12; Luke 11:4). The Amish of Pennsylvania practice forgiveness. They understand the command to forgive in order to receive forgiveness in terms of Matthew 18:23–35 and the parable of the man who begged the king to forgive him a debt of 10,000 talents, only to depart and immediately collar another man who owed him a hundred pence. The deed was reported to the king who threw the ungrateful miscreant into debtor's prison. Jesus concludes with this firmly starched warning: "So likewise shall my heavenly Father do also unto you, if ye from your hearts forgive not every one his brother their trespasses" (Matt 18:35, KJV). The initial forgiveness is free, but the continued and enduring forgiveness is conditional.[14] Jesus' parable is read every spring and fall in Amish church gatherings two weeks before the seasonal celebration of Communion Sunday and provides the interpretive context

---

13. Quoted in "Amish Grandfather: "We must not think evil of this man," *CNN.com*, October 4, 2006, accessed October 20, 2006.

14. Kraybill, Nolt, and Weaver-Zercher, *Amish Grace,* 89–90.

for the Lord's Prayer that we might be forgiven to the measure we forgive. Not a penny more, not a penny less.

David Steinmetz, the late professor of Christian history at Duke Divinity School and former resident of Lancaster County, Pennsylvania, wrote an editorial for the *News & Observer* in which he offered this explanation for the peculiar stance of the Amish people:

> The Amish forgave Roberts for imprisoning their children, for maiming and murdering them, and even for intending to molest them while they were helplessly in his power. They forgave him, not because he had been driven by private demons or because his act was anything but heinous. They forgave him because they thought Jesus had told them to and they were not clever enough to think he didn't mean it.[15]

Steinmetz made an important point: the Amish forgave not because Roberts's actions were forgivable, but because Jesus commanded his followers to forgive. It was not because Roberts could be excused for reasons of mental insanity or emotional instability, but because of Jesus. Forgiveness is not an option for the Christian, it is an order. One Amish man reacted in surprise and puzzlement at the national attention directed at the Amish habits of forgiveness—"Why is everybody all surprised?" he asked. "It's just standard Christian forgiveness; it's what everybody should be doing."[16]

Forgiveness, we should understand, does not equal pardon. In the act of forgiveness the person gives up the right to bear a grudge. It is the decision not to seek revenge or live in anger and resentment toward another person. Pardon is the action of the community. The community of Christ expects all members to extend forgiveness unconditionally even as the same community may or may not grant pardon to the wrongdoer. One remains accountable for one's actions and the consequences of those actions before the community. In some cases, the community may not even have authority to grant pardon. The Amish forgave Charles Roberts in their hearts and in public but they could not grant him pardon from his crimes—and not because he killed himself on that tragic day but because he was not a member of their church or subject to their *Ordnung*.[17] Forgiveness applies

---

15. David Steinmetz, "Forgiveness springs from their faith," *News & Observer*, October 18, 2006, newsobserver.com, accessed October 20, 2006.

16. Kraybill, Nolt, and Weaver-Zercher, *Amish Grace*, 49.

17. Ibid., 145–46.

to all while pardon derives from the rules, regulations, and procedures of a particular community.

All who submit to baptism submit their wills and desires, their fortunes and families, their ambitions and ways to the way of Christ and the leadership of his Spirit. With that comes the discipline of Christ in the unity of Christ's body, the church (Phil 2:2). In the case of a wayward member, the church may choose to release a person from the guilt and penalty of a wrongdoing if the member confesses, seeks pardon, undergoes discipline, or commits to reform and do differently. But if the individual refuses to submit to the discipline of the church community or to admit wrongdoing, then he or she may be shunned, removed from fellowship, excommunicated, or lose membership. Actions have consequences. And a major consequence of a disobedient or wrongful action is that the individual stands in need of forgiveness and submission to forgiveness. All Christians are called to forgive but to receive forgiveness is another matter. Here is an irony of life: many times it feels easier to offer forgiveness than accept it. The offending person must put aside pride, admit the need for forgiveness, and desire restoration and healing in order to receive the full effect and force of forgiveness (Matt 5:23–24). This is where the hard work begins.

The Politics of Bethlehem

Even on a superficial reading, the story of Jesus is a political one. Jesus endured trial and crucifixion under Pontius Pilate, the Roman procurator of the region. The crime posted over his head, "King of the Jews," the crime for which he was executed, was a political one. In the Gospels, the topic of Jesus' politics is ever-pressing. Sadducees, Pharisees, and political zealots quizzed his policies and positions. Jesus never gave them satisfactory answers. In the three synoptic Gospels, when Pilate questions Jesus about the accusations against him—that he claimed to be a king and to have a political agenda—Jesus refuses to answer or defend himself.[18] What is the reader to make of his silence? The Gospel of John provides some insight. When pressed by Pilate, Jesus replied, "My kingdom is not of this world. If my kingdom were of this world, my servants would have been fighting, that I might not be delivered over to the Jews. But my kingdom is not from the world" (John 18:36).

18. Matthew says he answered not a word (27:14). Mark and Luke record only that he said "You say that I am," which could be interpreted as a refusal to answer.

And so, the Gospel accounts twang with tightly wound tension between the political and the spiritual, the affairs of the world and the movements of heaven. The Gospels do not choose one over the other or arrange the two side by side in a neatly organized way. For these reasons, modern-day interpreters have difficulty drawing conclusions about these topics from the Gospels. The spheres of "religion" and "politics" did not exist as such for Jesus or the Gospel writers.[19] For Jesus and his disciples the world could not be compartmentalized into tidy little zones of religion, government, private belief, public discourse, entertainment, economics, and family life. These distinctions represent modern developments and post-Enlightenment ways of thinking. But in the Gospels such concerns are merged, or should we say they are not separated, so that the gospel's theology enables its politics just as its politics embodies its theology.

King of Kings

The town of Bethlehem itself provides an example of the way politics and faith cannot be dissociated in the Gospels. The story of Jesus begins with Joseph and Mary on the road, traveling the long stretch of road from home in Nazareth in Galilee to Bethlehem in Judea to oblige the requirements of the state. From the outset, the "religious" story of Jesus' life is set within a political context.

But, why would the parents travel the distance to their place of ancestral origin to accomplish the mundane task of registration? Roman law did not require they undertake such a journey. But Roman law did allow for local custom, the local custom in this case being ancestral registration.[20] So, perhaps they made the trip to the city of David's line because that's what local custom required. Despite what some commentators might think about this odd occurrence, a journey from Nazareth to Bethlehem right before the time of delivery, I would argue that it adds a measure of historicity to the event. Truth can be stranger than fiction. No one composing a fictionalized account of the birth narrative would have Mary and Joseph venture seventy miles from home only to arrive in scrawny Bethlehem.[21] Why not

19. Milbank, *Theology and Social Theory*, 1.

20. Brown, *Birth of the Messiah*, 549.

21. Archaeologists have identified another Bethlehem in the vicinity of Nazareth and proposed it as an alternative birth site. Unfortunately, this Bethlehem is in Galilee, not Judea as identified in the Gospels.

have them arrive in Jerusalem, the better known city of David and home to the holy Temple? It would seem that if the author were inventing the story of Jesus out of thin air, he would have him born in a more notable location. Barring that, the author could have at least saved some confusion and had Jesus the Nazarene delivered in Nazareth. That's how I would have written it. But that's exactly what makes the story as we have it all the more plausible. It doesn't follow pre-planned logic. It follows history.

Be that as it may, the young couple arrived in the city of David's birth for the registration. In this way, the story of Jesus is linked with that of David. David's reign represented the high-water mark of the Hebrew Scriptures and the golden age of Israel's history. Sacred history remembered him as a man after God's own heart and revered as a hero of his people. But first and foremost he was a king. Any association with David is always a political association. A birth in Bethlehem is by definition a political birth. And so the angelic heralds announced the arrival of a "savior" and "lord," the bringer of "peace" and "good will" (Luke 2:11–14), coincidentally all titles and descriptions used of the Roman Emperor.[22]

The first Roman to hold the role and office of emperor, not in name but certainly in authority, was Augustus, who ruled from 27 BC until his death in AD 14. He was not called "Emperor" in his own day. His birth name was Gaius Octavius but respectful subjects, colleagues, and citizens called him "Augustus," the "most revered one." The New Testament knows him as "Caesar Augustus."[23] Honored as a *divi filius*, or divine son, Caesar Augustus's birthday was celebrated as the birthday of a god. To quote from a document of the time, "the birthday of the god [Caesar Augustus] marked for the world the beginning of good tidings through his coming."[24] Augustus came bearing good news, and he himself was good news for the world. At one point, a high-ranking official, the proconsul of Asia, proposed beginning each year with Caesar Augustus's birthday, the twenty-third of September. After all, he said, the birth of the regal Augustus marked the beginning of all things including the "beginning of the breath of life" for all people.[25] Augustus restored law and order and purpose not only to

22. Green, *Gospel of Luke*, 134–35.

23. He took to himself the cognomen of his adoptive and murdered father, Julius Caesar, and the senate later conferred on him the title "Augustus." Everitt, *Augustus*, xi.

24. Price, *Rituals and Power*, 54

25. Paullus Fabius Maximus proposed this in the year 9 BC. Price, *Rituals and Power*, 54. Translation adapted from Johnson et al., eds., *Ancient Roman Statutes*, 119.

the Roman world, but for the ends of the earth. The birthday of Augustus stood for a new age that reversed the inevitable slide toward civil war and destruction. And so it seemed it ought be celebrated as a New Year's Day, a day on which the common good of all was dramatically improved.

Marble and bronze statues, temples, festivals, inscriptions, coins, honorific titles, and days of sacrifice all served to elevate the status of the Roman ruler to the height of divinity. But, where did he really come from? From Rome herself, the throbbing heart of the empire. Augustus's mother, Atia, gave birth to him at the family's Palatine residence close to the forum and senate house in Rome.[26] He was born and raised in the capital city. Surely the auspicious location of his birth presented itself as an omen of fortunes and power to come. The one born in the capital of the world would one day rule the world.

His father hailed from Velitrae (modern Velletri, Italy), a small city tucked like a field flower in the Alban hills, where the family had a villa and vineyard. Suetonius cites a prophecy from the town's history to lend some modicum of importance to the place. Once part of a wall in Velitrae was struck by lightning. The perplexed villagers took it as a sign that someone from there would one day rule the world.[27] This prophecy does not really aid Suetonius's case. It's rather paltry and unimpressive. Instead of elevating the town's mystique, the story has the reverse effect of making the town seem more quaint and homely. Given such humble material, bigger legends needed to be produced and circulated concerning Caesar Augustus's origin. Legend had it that his mother Atia once entered Velitrae's temple of Apollo in the witching hour of the night and fell asleep. While she slept a serpent attended her and left on her a scar that never fully disappeared. Nine months later she gave birth to the future ruler. Divine parentage was confirmed first to Atia through a dream and then later to Augustus through a similar dream in which the sun rose from Atia's womb.[28]

Of course, if there are any bragging rights in it, Jesus can claim humbler origins than Augustus. Although Jesus was born in the ancestral town of Israel's greatest king, his mother did not labor in the comfort of an estate in the capital city of Rome with nurse attendants at her side. Tradition assigns to Mary a rough-hewn cave that served as a simple animal shelter, a grotto. The grotto, which was known to Justin Martyr in the second century,

26. Everitt, *Augustus*, 7.

27. Suetonius, *Augustus* 94.2, 265–66.

28. Ibid. 94.4, 267. See also Dio, *Roman History* vol. 4 45.1–2.

Origen in the third, and Helena the mother of Constantine in the fourth, has since been lavishly decorated and fitted with a basilica of chapels. Aside from the rare but dramatic moments of conflict like the stand-off described above, the Basilica of the Nativity ordinarily plays host to thousands of pilgrims and visitors each day. Tourists report waiting in line up to two hours in order to pass by the grotto. By the time they reach it, they have endured flashing cameras, talking, shouting, eating, pushing, and bumping.

Originally, the place consisted of nothing more than a damp and dirty floor on which a poor couple could sit if they could endure the smell of the animals. And this is where the difference between Jesus and Caesar Augustus becomes clear. The contest is not whose origins was humbler. The question regards what should be made of those origins. The followers of Jesus embraced and adored the humble origins of the Messiah—as evidenced by the Basilica of the Nativity whereas the admirers of Augustus disdained his family's humble beginnings and did everything possible to disassociate him from the taint of the quotidian. The Romans turned the human Gaius Octavius into the divine Caesar Augustus while the Gospel writers practically humanized the divine Lord Jesus Christ into nothing more than a carpenter's son. In Jesus, God became one of us, even the poorest of us, to be loved and adored. In Augustus, the man Gaius Octavius became a god to be feared and revered, and most importantly, obeyed.

The superlative bolstering of Caesar Augustus's story masks its all-too-human ambition—to produce compliance and submission. The aim of the imperial cult, historians note, was not to establish an exclusive and all-encompassing religion, like Judaism or Christianity. In that regard, the aim was not religious at all. Instead, piety toward the ruler manifested loyalty to the regime. The "religion" of the emperor lacked any content other than to venerate, respect, and obey. Its purpose was self-evident.

In the births of Jesus and Augustus, then, we find parallel and contrast. The arrivals of both Jesus and Augustus mark the advent of a savior. Although each enters in humble obscurity, their births signal the beginnings of new epochs of peace and prosperity.[29] Each proclaims good news for folks far and wide. Each heralds a gospel or *euangelion*—a word that had political as well as religious currency. Mark, the earliest Gospel writer, introduces his story with the word *euangelion*, good tidings.[30] But the politics of Jesus contrasts sharply with the politics of Augustus, and by implication,

29. Basil, *Homily 27, Patrologia Graeca* 31:1473A.
30. Myers, *Binding the Strong Man*, 99–108.

the world. Jesus challenges the *libido dominandi*—that "desire to dominate" that puts a price on every soul (Mark 8:34—9:1) and grants to his disciples an authority far exceeding any earthly power: the power to bind and loose on earth and in heaven (Matt 18:18). He tells his followers not to worry about those who can kill the body only but do no further harm (Luke 12:4). He offers a peace that the world cannot match (John 14:27), and most importantly, he offers friendship (John 15:15).

It should be said that Augustus also offered friendship, *amicitia*. His was a friendship based on class and privilege and it did not extend far beyond the inner circle that ruled Rome. It was what the nobleman Symmachus called reverentially the sacred duty or "religion of friendship," *religio amicitiae*.[31] Jesus' friendship did not depend on influence, prestige, ancestry or income. "I do not call you servants [slaves] any longer, because the servant does not know what the master is doing; but I have called you friends, because I have made known to you everything that I have heard from my Father" (John 15:15).

Utopia

The prophecy that started this chapter, Micah's prophecy that peace and security will bubble up from the black ashes of Bethlehem and seep out to the ends of the earth, is a prophecy about friendship. Friendship is ultimately what Jesus brings. The Messiah insists that we no longer see each other as enemies to be avoided, outsmarted, or punished, but as friends to be released, reconciled, and handed a plate at the dinner table. The broad road is the one of crime and punishment, enemies and allies, law and order. The narrow road is the one of mediation and cooperation, listening and being heard, the chaos of forgiveness. If the Bedlam of hell means, in Micah's words, that God gives up, then heaven vows the opposite. The Eternal and Almighty One sticks with what he has made. The Good Shepherd refuses to abandon and walk away. Instead God makes peace, even at the expense of himself, so that we are not alone. And if we are to stay for any length of time in heaven, we must learn to forgive and make peace with those who injure us. That's the deal.

Where is God: in Rome or in Bethlehem? With the Emperor Augustus or with the baby Jesus? In the *quid pro quo* way of the world or in the dirt-path peace outside of Jerusalem? Bethlehem is in the world but not exactly

31. Brown, *Through the Eye of a Needle*, 101.

of the world. More than any place on earth, Bethlehem beckons an ideal, an impossibility, a *utopia* even. "Utopia" has become synonymous with irrational, unrealistic, and delusional. We speak of a utopian society as a pie-in-the-sky dream society. Most often the word appears on the heels of the adjective "impossible." That's unfortunate. Sir Thomas More (1478–1535), a deeply committed Christian who rose early to pray, ate minimally, and wore a hair shirt under his clothes as a sign of contrition, composed the short literary masterpiece entitled *Utopia*, from which we get the word, not as a weightless flight through the impossible but as a sharp censure of the decrepit economic systems and corrupt social institutions of his own day. More wrote in the vein of his friend Erasmus, the master of satire and social commentary, and understood well how his critiques would be received by those in power. "Do not you think," More has a character ask at one point in the book, "that if I were about any king, proposing good laws to him, and endeavouring to root out all the cursed seeds of evil that I found in him, I should either be turned out of his court, or, at least, be laughed at for my pains?"[32]

On More's island of Utopia, citizens show themselves to be productive but not greedy, proud but not classist, rational and not intolerant. They use communal property for the alleviation of social ills. The book *Utopia* appeared in 1516, just moments prior to the eruption of the Protestant Reformation and the concomitant dissolution of the Holy Roman Empire that would happen in the years to come. The wars of religion and the wars of nation-states, Protestantism, the Council of Trent, the Enlightenment, and modernity all lay in the future. And so, More's book appeared at a time when, culturally and politically speaking, anything was possible. The Renaissance period had reached its final peak and the time was such that proposals for novel and curious arrangements between society and economy could be taken seriously. The important twentieth-century Peruvian theologian, Gustavo Gutiérrez reminds us that More's fictitious island "in which the common good prevails, where there is no private property, no money or privileges, was the opposite of his own country, in whose politics he was involved."[33] In that sense, More created for his readers a city of the future, not a memory of the past. He did not want his readers to fly off to fairyland, nor did he want them to drift into a dream of Eden; he forged his ideals as tools to be implemented in real time. This, for Gutiérrez, is the

32. More, *Utopia*, 31.
33. Gutiérrez, *Theology of Liberation*, 135.

power of his work. For Gutiérrez, the utopian vision is always "subversive" of the ideologies of power and greed.[34]

If there be a silliness about Utopia, it is not the silliness of a society that shares all things in common and makes all members friends. Rather, it is the silliness of Utopia's opposite—the oxymoron of a society built on selfishness. For selfishness reverses society and greed knows no friends. If there be a biblical equivalent to the island of Utopia it is surely Bethlehem—the place where a child born in a stable can be king. And if we are to set our faces toward Bethlehem and our minds upon its utopian promise, then we must in the words of Phillips Brooks's beloved hymn ask the Lord Jesus to cast out our sin and enter in, and so be born in us today.

34. Ibid., 135.

Charting Stars

Of all the historical markers that locate Jesus' birth, the most prominent is the star that "stopped over the place where the child was" (Matt 2:9). In comparison to the other pieces of information about the timing of the event, the star shines forth as the brightest. For this reason, we must give special consideration to the biblical, historical, and theological significance of the heavenly orb spotted by the wise men from the east.[1]

Symbols of Light

Let us begin with the symbol of the star's light. Christmas is a season of light, or, more exactly, Christmas emphasizes light during what is otherwise a long spell of short days and extended hours of darkness. The hymns of the church testify to it. "Let All Mortal Flesh Keep Silence," from the fifth century *Liturgy of St. James,* proclaims the Light of light descending at the incarnation. The triumphant "Hark! The Herald Angels Sing" by Charles Wesley hails the Sun of righteousness, proclaiming light and life to all he brings. "Go, Tell It on the Mountain" witnesses a holy light that shone throughout the heavens. William Neidlinger's twentieth-century ditty sings of a bright sky on the holy night that was, after all, the birthday of a King. And finally, we must mention the imagery of light heard in the most beloved Christmas carol of all time: Joseph Mohr and Franz Gruber's *Stille*

---

1. The University of Groningen, Netherlands, brought together nineteen experts from fields such as astronomy, ancient history, religion, biblical studies, and culture for a three-day colloquium on the subject in 2014. See Barthel and Kooten, eds., *Star of Bethlehem.*

Nacht, "Silent Night," first performed on the eve of Christmas, 1818, in the town of Oberndorf near Salzburg. In it we witness shadows of darkness fly and all become light.

Many notable carols go beyond the contrast of light and dark by identifying the source of light in the night sky, the *star*. These include "The First Noel," "Carols Sing," "Gentle Mary Laid Her Child," "Sing We Now of Christmas," and "As with Gladness Men of Old." Timothy Dudley-Smith's gentle lullaby, "Away in a Manger," describes the stars in the sky (plural) looking down where the baby lay. The kid-friendly tune "Do You Hear What I Hear?" imagines a star dancing in the night with a tail as big as a kite. Other carols describe how the star reflected off clouds and hills and directed the feet of shepherds and wise men.

The star has inspired countless composers. Yet, the star does nothing more than flash the way toward the true source of brightness—the Christ child. The stately and dignified carol "We Three Kings of Orient Are," re-members this. After lauding the star with royal beauty bright, "We Three Kings" asks that the westward leading star guide us to the perfect light—Je-sus. Christina Rossetti's "Love Came Down at Christmas" likewise reminds us that the star is a sign of Christ's truth. James Montgomery's nineteenth-century classic, "Angels, from the Realms of Glory," calls it the infant's star. From the sixteenth century, Philipp Nicolai praises the "Morning Star" beaming forth in truth and light. Nicolai equates the Bethlehem star with the astronomical morning star, Venus, in order to draw a theological com-parison to Christ. Such a comparison was first made by 2 Peter 1:19. The imagery is powerful, for at certain times of the year Venus "rises" a few hours before the sun as a bright and brilliant morning star, so Peter speaks of Christ the morning star rising in our hearts, marking the dawn of a new day. The new day is the kingdom of God and the restoration of creation.

In the divine liturgy of Byzantine churches, a cloth is placed over the host bread of communion. The cloth is in the shape of a six-pointed star of David. The priest drapes it over the host and echoes the words of Matthew 2:9, "And behold, a star came and stood over where the Child was," signify-ing that under the star cloth is the presence of the son of David and Son of God. In many churches, both Protestant and Roman, the symbolism of the star and of light is incorporated into the use of an Advent wreath.

The wreath consists of five candles, three taper candles of purple, one rose (or pink), and one white pillar in the center, which is lit last. Each Sunday of Advent another candle is lit. With each new candle adding its light, the brightness grows. When all the candles are burning at once, it is clear that the wreath is above all else a symbol of light.

Within this wreath of light, each candle symbolizes something different. The first, a purple candle, speaks of hope, expectation, and the messianic prophecies of the Old Testament. The second purple candle represents Gabriel's annunciation to Mary. The third taper stands out because it is rose-colored. It symbolizes joy and rejoicing and is lit on Gaudete Sunday at the midway point of Advent's journey to Christmas. The final purple taper adds its light on the fourth Sunday, purple being a color of penance and preparation for the great mystery of the incarnation. The center white pillar is saved until Christmas and dramatizes the anticipation of Christ's arrival, the light of the world.

Evergreen and holly are used to create the circle of the wreath. These keep their color all year and so symbolize the everlasting life in Christ. Sometimes pine cones, berries, and seedpods are used to decorate the wreath, and these too have meaning—representing rebirth and renewal. They signify resurrection. The seeds and pods dropped into winter's hard-packed earth represent nature's promise of new life to come in warmer weather. To us they also speak of the Holy Spirit's promise that the dead in Christ will be raised on the last day. From death and burial springs life. So it is in God's created order. The same God who created the seasonal rhythms of death and rebirth also created us for resurrection after death.

I don't wish to give the impression that the Advent wreath and its candles have only one meaning and only one form. Any number of variations on the Advent wreath have been tested and tried and any number of meanings have been proposed—a fact that is hardly surprising given that churches all over the world light the wreath. It should also be remembered that the tradition itself trails back far into Christian history and can even trace roots to the pre-Christian practices of the Scandinavian and Germanic peoples. Churches should be encouraged to incorporate and adapt the candle wreaths to their own contexts. This is how traditions stay alive.

Gazing at the Sky

A common scenery element found in a crèche or nativity set is the star suspended above the thatched roof of the animal shelter where the baby lay, conveniently creating an ornamental and artistic center to the scene. In sketches and paintings, the star usually operates like a stadium spotlight focusing its beam down on the stage and illuminating shepherds, donkeys, camels, wise men, Mary, Joseph, and especially the baby. Although the star has become a standard element of the modern-day nativity scene, it seems that at the time of Jesus' birth the only ones to notice it were foreigners from the east. Their enthusiasm, as strong as it was, was theirs alone.

We are given precious few details about the magi. Martin Luther confesses, "How these magi recognized this star to be such a sign which certainly signified a new born king, I do not know."[2] We are only informed that they came from the east bearing gifts of gold, frankincense, and myrrh. One medieval legend said they also gave the baby Jesus a wine goblet which would later be used at the last supper—the Holy Grail. Notwithstanding this legend, their gifts were three in number, and so tradition presumed the wise men numbered three. Such strange and exotic characters could not be left undescribed. Tradition soon gave them names—Balthasar, Melchior, and Gaspar. They were also given appearances. One would be black or African, one Asian or Persian, and one Middle Eastern, representing the global reach of the gospel message to all peoples of every nation. One would be depicted as a child, another as an adult, and the third an elderly gentleman, expressing the conviction that the gospel message applies to all people of all ages and all times.

Directors of church drama productions are eternally grateful to the wise men, for they have given the greatest gift of all—the gift of brightly colored costumes. In church nativity plays, the wise men in luxurious and glittering costumes add color and festivity to an otherwise monochromatic brown and tan wardrobe. The magi appear strange and exotic. At times their outfits and demeanor border on the outlandish and preposterous, so it is no surprise that drama productions cast them as comic relief. The nativity provides precious few moments of humor, and so they play the part of the clown.

Whatever their original dress or deportment, the magi deserve credit for discovering a new star. It was their job to watch the dome of the sky for celestial movements, and they saw something that had caused them to pack their bags and head west.

But, what is the biblical significance of the star? Let's start by looking at something written by Eusebius of Caesarea, a highly educated and intellectually gifted man of his age. Eusebius extolled the astronomical sign of the new star as the worldwide herald of the incarnation.

2. Luther, Gospel for the Festival of the Epiphany, in *Sermons II*, 169.

In the case of remarkable and famous men we know that strange stars have appeared, what some call comets, or meteors, or tails of fire, or similar phenomena that are seen in connexion with great or unusual events. But what event could be greater or more important for the whole universe than the spiritual light coming to all men through the saviour's advent, bringing to human souls the gift of holiness and the true knowledge of God? Wherefore the herald star gave the great sign, telling in symbol that the Christ of God would shine as a great new light on all the world.[3]

Eusebius connected the star over Bethlehem with the prophecy of Balaam in Numbers 24. And this in particular makes his statement interesting.

Balak, the wicked king of Moab, plotted to destroy Moses and his dusty-footed people. Knowing that the Israelites had the protection of a powerful divinity, Yahweh, Balak decided to enlist supernatural powers of his own. He hired from the east a certain diviner named Balaam, called a *magus* by Philo of Alexandria, to rain down curses upon Israel. Balaam consented but when the time arrived to let the curses fly, he failed the terms of his agreement miserably. Try as he might, Balaam could not curse Israel. Instead, he blinked, squinted, and related these stunned words to Balak: "I see him, but not now; I behold him, but not near." And then, as if rubbing his eyes into focus, Balaam said, "a star shall come out of Jacob, and a scepter shall rise out of Israel" (Num 24:17). And what might this star do? Balaam delivered the unwelcomed news to Balak. It would bring down a crushing blow upon Moab, Seth, Edom, Seir, Ir, and all the rest.

We can only imagine the shock and consternation Balaam and Balak experienced at these words. Israel had not been cursed like Balak wanted because Balaam was unable to do it. Far from predicting Israel's ruin, Balaam foresaw the obliteration of Israel's enemies.

As fascinating as this story is, New Testament commentators are drawn to it for another reason. They wonder why Matthew, who is usually keen to connect Jesus events to Hebrew prophecies, fails to reference this prophecy. Matthew does not cite Balaam's prophecy, despite the fact that Matthew is the one who relates the new star rising over the child. Even so, Balaam's prophecy anticipates Christ, as Eusebius rightly understands.[4] According to Eusebius, Balaam spoke of things "that would be accomplished

3. Eusebius, *Demonstratio evangelica* 9.1, p. 419.

4. See Helen Jacobus, "Balaam's 'Star Oracle' in the Dead Sea Scrolls and Bar Kokhba," in Barthel and Kooten, eds., *Star of Bethlehem*, 399–431.

a very long time after his own day."[5] Balaam drew a line from a new star on the dome of the heavens to a new ruler rising in Israel. Eusebius draws the line directly to Christ, whose kingship extended beyond Israel to the world.

Neither Balaam nor Eusebius could be counted as the first to observe this kind of astrological connection. The appearance or disappearance of a heavenly body was taken by everyone in the ancient world to portend a significant birth. It was common knowledge. Scholars at Alexandria and Pergamum wrote serious handbooks on such matters and astrologers observed new stars with the births of the Roman emperors Alexander Severus and Marcus Aurelius's son Commodus. Streaking comets and new stars marked the conception and ascension of Mithridates VI Eupator of Pontus. Legendary accounts in Judaism of the birth of Abraham and later, in Islam of the birth of Mohammed, mentioned the rising of new lights in the night sky. One star fell at the birth of Lao-Tze. The historian Tacitus reported "the general belief is that a comet means a change of emperor" while Pliny the Elder observed that the brightness or dimness of the star often corresponded to the prosperity or poverty of the individual.[6]

A medieval folktale still relished in Italian households to this day is the legend of la Befana. There is no single literary source for the story of la Befana; like all good folk traditions, it exists in countless variations and suggests any number of meanings.

In most retellings of the story, Befana appears as an unfriendly old woman whose back is perpetually bent over her broom while she sweeps the house. From under her door passersby catch whiffs of something delicious baking in the oven. No one knows what it might be because Befana never lets anyone in. She is forever preparing to receive guests but is too grouchy and inhospitable to actually do so. In other versions of the story, Befana comes across as a kind and generous grandmother who always entertains guests but never stops to rest. Either way, one night a knock at the door rouses her from bed. The three wise men stand before her house asking for directions to the Christ child. In some accounts she provides them lodging for the night. In other accounts she shoos them away. The tale reaches its climax when the exotic travelers extend the hand of friendship and ask her to join them in their search for the newborn baby. She apologizes, waving her broom around at all the housework yet to be done and says she cannot

---

5. Eusebius, *Demonstratio evangelica* 9.1, p. 419.

6. Tacitus, *Annals* 14.22; Pliny, *Natural History* 2.28. Davies and Allison, *Matthew* vol. 1, 233–34.

go. The wise men leave, and no sooner are they gone than Befana changes her mind. She hurries out the door but cannot find them. To this day she searches for the Christ child, visiting every house where children sleep. She always carries her broom, and she sometimes uses it to sweep the houses she visits and other times to swat the children. On account of her broom, modern-day Italians refer to her as a witch.

Her story is usually remembered on Epiphany, the sixth of January.[7] In the church calendar, Epiphany celebrates Christ's baptism and the moment when John the Baptist and the crowds see the dove descending and hear the voice from heaven. In that moment, everyone begins to realize Jesus' true identity. Befana, of course, is doomed to miss it and to wander endlessly in search of the Christ.

Innumerable permutations of this basic folktale get told by animated storytellers.[8] The lessons remain more or less the same. One is hospitality, not getting so focused on the cleanliness of the house or the chores of the day that you miss the relationships and the gentle signs from God. La Befana illustrates well the moral of the Gospel story of Martha. Luke tells us that this unbelievably fortunate woman had Jesus under the very roof of her house, but alas, she was too preoccupied with her housework to notice. Martha even chastised her sister Mary for sitting at the feet of Jesus and not helping her with the meal preparations. Jesus famously answered Martha's frustration, "Martha, dear Martha, you're fussing far too much and getting yourself worked up over nothing. One thing only is essential, and Mary has chosen it—it's the main course, and won't be taken from her" (Luke 10:41–42, *The Message*). If the parable of the bridesmaids whose lamps run out of oil reminds us to be prepared, then the stories of Martha and Befana remind us not to obsess over those same preparations.

"Seek the Lord while he may be found" (Isa 55:6), for there may come a time when the star fades or hides behind a cloud.

---

7. The name "Befana" may derive from the Italian word for the feast of the Epiphany on January 6, *Epifania* and *la festa dell'Epifania*, but the figure of Befana may be traced back to pre-Christian spirits and traditions.

8. See, for instance, de Paola, *Legend of Old Befana*. There are also a number of different ways to remember la Befana. Italian parents will slip a lump of coal in the form of dark sugar candy into the stockings of children on the eve of Epiphany and say it is from Befana. They will also tell the children that they would get presents if they were good all year long, but who could possibly do that? In Urbania and throughout the Umbrian region, grand festivals are held to celebrate the witch with plenty of opportunities to buy candies and sweetbreads and straw broomsticks.

Star Appearances

We have considered the star from a couple of angles, but we still need to explore what it represents theologically. For one, the star over Bethlehem announced the approach of a new power. This was in fact Jesus' first message in Galilee: "Repent, for the kingdom of heaven has come near" (Matt 4:17; Mark 1:15). Again and again throughout his ministry Jesus announced the kingdom of heaven—that it has come near, that it is not far, that it has come to you, that it is among you (Matt 10:7, 12:28; Mark 12:34; Luke 10:9, 11:20, 17:21). The star speaks of the nearness of the kingdom, which speaks of the nearness of heaven, which speaks of the presence of the Lord, which is the Gospel message. Like the light from a small beacon on the nose of a colossal cruise ship, the Judean star acts as the tiny but visible tip of something much larger gliding behind it: the kingdom of heaven.

The incarnation of God's Son on earth is heralded by the appearance of a new star in the heavens. But, the *appearance* of a new star is not the same thing as the *creation* of a new star. The appearance of a new star in our night sky does not mean that a new star has suddenly come into existence. The appearance of a new star in the heavens signifies that the light from a star millions of light years away has just now reached our eyes. The star itself has existed for ages and the light that has traveled across endless empty space to announce its presence is very old. It has traveled a very long time. Our own galaxy is 100,000 light years across, so even within our own galaxy, light from a new star can take 10,000 years to reach us. The farthest objects we can see by telescope are quasars, which are so distant from us that the light we see today from them was emitted billions of years ago. The star over the land of Judea might have been born hundreds of thousands of years before its appearance in the night sky. But here it appeared, at just the right moment, at just the point in history when the babe who would change history was born in Bethlehem.

That is to say, the light of God was on its way long before entering Mary's womb. It had been traveling since before Mary had been born, since before Mary's mother had been born, since before Solomon or Ruth or Joshua or Miriam had been born. God set the plan in motion before the beginning of time. The plan had always been Jesus. This the star announced. Heaven bent close to earth and the grand universe of God's design grazed nearer than we could imagine, nearer to us than we are to our own hearts.

I grew up in the arid border town of El Paso, Texas, a place of rugged moonlike vistas and few trees. In spite of this, it remains for me a landscape of the heart. The city has two natural boundaries: the tiny but persistent Rio Grande that flows from north to south dividing the United States and Mexico, and a brawny mountain ridge known as Mount Franklin that divides the city. El Paso conforms itself around the two sides of the mountain. We lived on the west side, but at Christmastime we would load into the old brown and tan family van and ride to the east side at sunset.

Interstate 10, the superhighway that stretches from California to Florida, connects El Paso's west and east sides like a stringy tendon hinging two muscle groups on either side of a bone. We did not take that way though, preferring the older and less trafficked Transmountain Drive that took a gradual ascent up the west side of Mt. Franklin. On the unlit bend around Smuggler's Pass, one could forget about the teeming city of half a million people below. The road cut and curved over the mountain, making a sharp descent down the east side. And this is why we came, to look over our shoulders and out the windows at the east side of the mountain whose ridges in the dark looked like the body of a slumbering giant covered by a thin bed sheet. We looked for the star. It was not hard to find. At night *la estrella grande* presided majestically over the low-rise, sun-bleached subdivisions below. The star formation I marveled at as a child was created by a series of light bulbs stretching almost 500 feet and laid at a 30 degree angle on the side of the mountain. It is visible from 100 miles in the air and 30 miles on land. To my childhood eyes the star looked for all the world like it came directly from Bethlehem. I wondered if this was what the magi saw and why they were drawn irresistibly to the spot where the child lay.

My memory of the El Paso star tastes and smells of wonder and delight. It impressed upon me a sense of comfort and assurance that everything would be okay. And this, I believed, was what the Bethlehem star must have communicated to the shepherds and the wise men. It was for them an unmistakable sign of joy and hope illuminating the way.

As I grew older and thought about it, I realized there was more at work in the symbol of the star. The nearness of a star's light, or at least the sense of nearness we get from seeing the light of a star, masks the distance of the star from us. The Bethlehem star represents the nearness of the kingdom of heaven but at the same time it represents the distance of the kingdom of heaven. Nietzsche's madman gets it right: "Big events take time, lightning and thunder take time, the light of stars takes time, deeds take time, both before and after they are done, to be seen and heard."[9] The coming of God's

9. Nietzsche, *Gay Science*, §125, p. 182.

Son to earth for our salvation should be the loudest and brightest spectacle known to humans, but it often feels farther from us than the farthest star. It has already happened, God has already come to earth, already revealed his plan and his love. Jesus has already died and been raised, the day has already been saved. And yet the people of the world are not fully aware of it, not sufficiently awake to the fact. Like people accustomed to the dark and thrust into a well-lit room, they close their eyes, shield their faces, and stumble about blindly. Light has on them the same effect as darkness. From the perspective of the blind, light is just another form of darkness. And to those unaccustomed to using their eyes, darkness is to be preferred because it is less painful than the brilliance of brightness.

Matthew's gospel reports that only the magi were able to decipher the meaning of the new star over Israel. For the most part, we think of the star as big and luminous and blinking directly over the manger with the efficiency of a movie attendant's flashlight, but this notion comes from illustrated Christmas cards and paintings. The star did not, in point of fact, function like a low-slung traffic sign for all to see and follow. If that was the case, then it did its job poorly because only a couple of stargazers noticed it.[10] What does it mean, then, that the star remained a mystery to everyone except a few professionals from the east? This question leads me to suspect that the star not only pointed to the closeness of the event, but also, and more importantly, to its distance.

The star of Bethlehem symbolizes longing. It represents the heaven before our eyes but just beyond our grasp. It represents the hope of Saint Paul for the resurrection of bodies and the union of souls with Christ in the air on the last day. It signifies hope and suggests what Thomas Merton called the *point vierge*, the virgin point just before the morning sun ruptures the horizon, scattering birdsong and morning mist.[11] Insofar as it symbolizes hope, it also symbolizes unfulfillment. It is a sign that we are not in heaven, that we have not attained the resurrection, that our bodies have not yet been redeemed (Rom 8:23–5). We stand between the times, residents of no time really. We inhabit the *saeculum*—an old Latin word from which we get our word "secular." But at its root, *saeculum* connotes more than the word "secular" can indicate. It describes the long duration of

10. In Matthew's telling, it seems that the star that guided the magi to Jerusalem vanished so that the magi had to inquire at Herod's court. Then, "there, ahead of them, went the star that they had seen at its rising, until it stopped over the place where the child was" (Matt 2:9).

11. Merton, *Guilty Bystander*, 131–32.

worldliness where we live now. We occupy a secular time, that is, a strange stretch of twilight before the end of things.

Heavens Alight

The new light in the heavens indicated to the Persian magi that heaven itself had taken an interest in the livelihood of humankind. Mulling over this star created in them and in us a powerful desire to know more. We want to touch, taste, and see more of this heaven hinted at by the twinkling orb in the sky.

What can we say?

No artist, poet, philosopher, or theologian in the history of the world has ever done justice to heaven. The rickety words of human beings jump the rails and crash at the border of paradise. Why? Is it because we lack descriptive powers sufficient to the task? Possibly. But it seems that a more galling shortcoming of human nature might be to blame. Perhaps it is our innate inability to get over our own seriousness.

After the whips and claws of hell's black furnace, the clouds and harps of heaven seem to us—how should we say it—a bit trifling. We can't help it. After Dante's screaming descent down the everlasting rings of inferno with Lucifer gnawing at the bodies of Brutus, Judas, and Cassius, his visit to the cool gardens and palaces of heaven strikes the reader as anticlimactic. Dante depicts the red-orange scenes of Hades in vivid detail, but of heaven's delights he can only pardon himself, "I am like one, who sees in dream, and when the dream is gone an impression, set there, remains, but nothing else comes to mind again, since my vision almost entirely fails me."[12]

Really? Nothing comes to mind?

Theologically, this is probably as it should be. The gates of hell swing tantalizingly within the grasp of human imagination. But the Bethlehem star remains just out of reach. Heaven sits just beyond our line of sight. Every depiction of heaven that I have seen in film, in art, or in a worship setting, contains an element of farce. None escape the "cheese" factor completely. All give off a smarmy, sentimental, fake feeling. No matter how bold the picture or beautiful the poetry, it is hard to shake corniness of golden-winged baby-fat cherubs, billowy white clouds, slow-motion smiles, and Saint Peter checking an ID at the gate.

What can we do if not laugh about it?

12. Dante, *Paradiso*, Canto 33, 49–145.

Attempts to picture it do not inspire awe and wonder as much as they manifest the ridiculousness of the attempt. In fact, any attempt to conjure heaven on earth might as well be the "penguin house."[13] Back in 2004 Paul Craig decided to turn his modest Olathe, Kansas home and yard into a penguin-themed holiday bonanza. Every year over 150 lighted and air-filled vinyl fabric penguin creations get crammed into the residential quarter-acre lot. Visitors are welcome on the property, but they must squeeze past one another in the few open spaces between inflatables. No square inch survives undecorated. Even the roof, where inflated objects do not fare well in the wind, displays a huge screen that runs penguin-themed movies. We took our daughter Cassidy to it when she was elementary school age and she was mesmerized by the place.

The penguin house is one of the most popular displays in the Kansas City metro area but it's surely no heaven. It doesn't pretend to the sublime or the profound. Even so, maybe the penguin house can teach us something about all human efforts to capture the sublimity and profundity of heaven—they fall short, woefully short. They might as well be penguin houses.

I am always humbled when I think of Saint Paul's analogy of the resurrection and eternal life. In 1 Corinthians 15, Paul compares this present existence to the everlasting life of the resurrection of the Lord—it is a seed next to the majestic tree that sprouted from the seed. In terms of appearance, the two share nothing in common: the hard, black, slick nut of a seed; the roots, trunk, branches, bark, and leaves of the tree. And yet, they share the same essential DNA instruction manual. So it is, Paul says, between our present selves and our future selves, between the world that is and the world to come. "What is sown is perishable, what is raised is imperishable. It is sown in dishonor, it is raised in glory. It is sown in weakness, it is raised in power. It is sown a physical body, it is raised a spiritual body" (1 Cor 15: 42–44). God has embedded within us and within the world all that is to be, but we do not see it. We are but seeds. This is the difference between earth and heaven.

Mute Announcements

A star may exist for eons without its light being visible to our planet. Just because its light has not yet reached our atmosphere does not mean it does not yet exist. And although we cannot see it, its light rockets towards our planet

---

13. Technically it is Paulie's Penguin Playground, but locals call it the penguin house.

at 186,000 miles per second, the speed of light. When its light reaches us, astronomers announce its arrival. But in truth, they are announcing what already is and has been for some time—the "new" star has been burning for thousands and thousands of years. Its distance from us has prevented us from knowing about it. So, Christians act like astronomers, but of a more spectacular kind. We announce that Jesus Christ is the world's Savior and true King. This is an odd claim because it is not exactly demonstrable or self-evident. It is a claim, so we believe and confess, on which Christ has already made good even though at present it remains unseen and unrealized. Christ has already done what he was sent to do, the work is finished, but the gospel light is still on its way and has yet to reach our eyes. Heaven has already appeared and yet our eyes see earth only. For now, without such sight, we walk by faith.

We announce Christ with the confidence of faith but also with the anticipation of hope. As Isaiah 9:2 prophesied:

> The people walking in darkness
>   have seen a great light;
> on those living in the land of deep darkness
>   a light has dawned.

Even before the light of the world is revealed, its coming is hinted at and anticipated. The words of Isaiah about a light shining on those who sit in darkness appear in Luke 1:79, in the exuberant speech of Zechariah, a priest well-versed in the Scriptures. Named after the Old Testament prophet, it must be said that Zechariah fell short of his namesake. When an angel alerted him to the impending birth of a son, his faith was found wanting. The Bible reports his doubts and their consequences. Although there is nothing in Zechariah's response to the angel's announcement to suggest he was anything but baffled and perplexed—"How will I know that this is so? For I am an old man, and my wife is getting on in years" (Luke 1:18)—the angel saw past the words of his mouth to the meditations of his heart. Mercifully, we do not know what the angel saw. Did Zechariah doubt? Was there a smirking incredulity behind his question? Did his tone somehow reveal a deep-seated sense of self-importance? Did he harbor a desperate need to be always in control of the situation? From this distance we cannot say.

Lightning-fast, the messenger of the Lord rendered Zechariah mute—he would remain that way until his son was born. And again, we can only imagine what Zechariah must have thought about during those long days of mute silence leading up to his son's birth. What regrets? What justifications? What explanations to his wife and others who wondered why he could not speak? What we do know is that when the vice grip holding his tongue finally loosened on the day of John's birth, Zechariah let out this proclamation:

> By the tender mercy of our God,
>> the dawn from on high will break upon us,
> to give light to those who sit in
>> darkness and in the shadow of death,
> to guide our feet into the way of peace (Luke 1:78–9).

Of all people, Zechariah knew something about the natural human tendency to disbelieve. He had personally suffered the consequences of faithless skepticism. He knew that human nature prefers to creep unnoticed in the dark and curl up with the shadows of death. Left to our own devices, we will not find God or peace or meaning. We do not rotate the earth until we face the sun, rather, we lie in darkness while the earth goes around on its own accord. The sun must find us. The light must dawn on us. Salvation is not our work but God's.[14] Zechariah eventually learned this lesson and taught it to his son, John, who made straight the way of the Lord and became less so that he might become more.

The star of Bethlehem speaks of the closeness and distance of God. It speaks to the flat-headed fact that we do not find God on our own. We must be shown the way, we must be told, we must be led by the hand through the dark to the grace of light.

---

14. Luther observes that the star goes before the magi and does not leave them until it brings them to Christ, so the bright lamp of the gospel does not leave us until it brings us to Christ. *Sermons II,* 274.

Jesus the Migrant

Picture Joseph and Mary's escape to Egypt. See Joseph snapping awake at the angel's words in his ear—"Get up!" Panicked, he shakes Mary from her sleep. In the darkness they pack their spare belongings—a handful of clay water jars and blankets. Mary scoops up their most precious possession—a baby boy—and bundles him tight. Without a word they duck through the door of their low-slung abode. Joseph doesn't look back. The family disappears into the night.

Herod on the Loose

This is not the story's beginning. We must leave for a moment Mary and Joseph's scrambling departure to watch the fanciful arrival of an exotic entourage at the court of King Herod. Matthew's gospel identifies the arriving strangers as magi from the east. One can only imagine what they looked like, what they wore, how they spoke, what their manner of behavior must have been. Herod folded his hands politely and composed himself to receive the outlandishly dressed foreigners. The travelers bowed in deference and stated their purpose for the visit in the form of a question, "Where is the child who has been born king of the Jews? For we observed his star at its rising, and have come to pay him homage" (Matt 2:2–3).

Herod glanced around curiously. Was this a joke? No one was laughing. Had he heard the magi correctly? Had something been lost in translation? No. They were looking for a child. He must have then wondered if he had a mistress or wife he had forgotten. Who was this child who was supposed to be his? "When King Herod heard this, he was frightened, and all Jerusalem with him" (Matt 2:23).

It is an understatement to say that Herod the Great was not well loved by the people during his long thirty-three year–rule over Palestine. The ordinary people hated him.[1] The Roman senate granted him the title "King of the Jews" and he followed Jewish religious customs scrupulously, but people still questioned the legitimacy of his Jewishness due to his Idumean extraction. He undertook new building campaigns for the betterment of the province, including the rebuilding of the Jerusalem Temple, and earned the moniker "Great," but his savage cruelty clouded any gratitude and devotion he might have enjoyed from his subjects. And so, Herod the Great lived in constant fear of plots afoot to unthrone him. He put first wife, Mariamme, to death on suspicion of treason. After that he took in marriage nine other wives. By his legitimate wives he had fifteen children. He likely had other mistresses and sons about whom we have no record. As the number of his wives and children increased, so did his paranoia. Herod was no family man. He so feared usurpation by his sons that he had three of them pre-emptively executed.

All of this is to say that when Herod heard the announcement of the magi from the east bringing greetings and tidings of a new birth, he panicked. The fearful response recorded in Matthew is fully consistent with his character and his typical pattern of behavior. He may well have assumed that the child about which the magi spoke was indeed his own—a legitimate or illegitimate son that had been concealed from his knowledge. Whether the child had a hereditary connection with him or not, Herod decided in his mind what he would do. He would not permit any potential contender for the throne to live.

Herod commanded the magi to return and report their findings on the pretext that he too might go and pay respects. Herod, so the text tells us, had no intention of worshipping the newborn king, but of ridding his kingdom of any future claimant.

Did Matthew know of the parallel between his own story and that told by Herodotus? According to Herodotus's *Histories*, Astyages, king of the Medes, consulted eastern magi in order to ascertain the clear meaning of his dreams. The magi informed him that the dreams indicated that the son recently born to his daughter and her Persian husband would one day

---

1. Marshak, *Many Faces of Herod the Great.*

be king. King Astyages responded in the manner of Herod and sought to eliminate the child.[2]

In the Gospels, the magi proved themselves wise in more ways than one. They paid homage to the baby and his parents in private, presenting gold, frankincense, and myrrh, and then, having been warned in a dream, they left the country by another way, eluding Herod (Matt 2:12). Herod's reaction to this slight from the magi must be characterized as nothing less than a temper tantrum. "When Herod saw that he had been tricked by the wise men, he was infuriated, and he sent and killed all the children in and around Bethlehem who were two years old or under" (Matt 2:16). The Roman historian Suetonius reports a similar occurrence: in the months before the birth of Gaius Octavius, the future emperor known to us as Caesar Augustus, there came a portent that nature herself was pregnant with the future king of the Romans, "thereupon the senate in consternation decreed that no male child born that year should be reared."[3] Suetonius also reports that the pregnant women of the city saw to it that the order was not enacted for the reason that each mother believed that the portent applied to herself. Assuming that Herod the Great was more successful in enacting his decree upon the residents of Bethlehem than the senate of Rome, how many lives are we talking about?

The death count is much higher in our minds than it must have been in real life. We imagine it to be in the thousands. Roman Catholic, Anglican, Lutheran, and other Protestant churches commemorate the Holy Innocents three days after Christmas, on the twenty-eighth of December,[4] and when we attend a church service or Mass dedicated to the Holy Innocents, we cannot help but wonder about the number of children who died and assume it must have been high to warrant a feast day in the liturgical calendar. Taking a cue from Revelation 14:3, the Greek liturgy sets the figure at 144,000. In reality it must have been much less. The population of Bethlehem at the time can be estimated at somewhere between 300 and 1,000 people. Given that the total population did not exceed a thousand, there could not have been more than ten to twenty children under the age

---

2. Herodotus, *Histories* 1.204.

3. Suetonius, *Augustus*, 94.3, p. 266.

4. Some traditions observe December 27 (Western and Eastern Syrians) or December 29 (Orthodox).

of two.[5] The death count might have been as few as five or six.[6] Given such a small number of victims, the deed would have gone unnoticed by most. A single detachment of men could have carried out Herod's order swiftly. No one other than the stunned parents needed to know what happened. Little wonder that Josephus did not record the event in his chronicle.

The crime is no less horrific for its small numbers. The inhabitants remembered the nightmare and sang the lament of Jeremiah with "wailing and loud lamentation"—the sound of the mother "weeping for her children" who are no more (Jer 31:15; Matt 2:18). The murder of even one child is a terrible and shameful thing—so much more shameful the murder of six or ten or twenty.

Our modern sensitivities about babies force us to suspect the reliability of this story—surely Herod did not command such a horrendous sacrifice? No one would be that heartless, right?

Sadly, Herod was more than capable of such barbarity. He did not spare his own wife or sons, or anyone suspected of betraying him. When he entered Jerusalem by force, he put to death forty-five men from among those who had opposed him as a warning for others.[7] When an assassination plot that involved ten men was uncovered, the men and their families and the families of those who helped them were tortured and executed. On another occasion, he demanded that all inhabitants of the region swear allegiance to the Roman Caesar and to himself as their rightful ruler. A faction of 6,000 Pharisees refused and were fined. The fine was paid by a certain wealthy woman identified as Pheroras' wife. "In return for her friendliness they [the Pharisees] foretold—for they were believed to have foreknowledge of things through God's appearance to them—that by God's decree Herod's throne would be taken from him, both from himself and his descendants, and the royal power would fall to her and Pheroras and to any children that they might have."[8] Herod's fury boiled over into violence. The Pharisees who had made these predictions were executed, as were individuals from Herod's own household who believed the prophecies, including Bagoas and Karos.

Whereas the wise men took gifts, Herod took lives.

5. France, *Gospel of Matthew*, 85.
6. Hahn, *Joy to the World*, 137.
7. Josephus, *Jewish Antiquities* 25.5.
8. Ibid. 17.43, p. 393.

With this background information about Herod in mind, we return to the angel's nighttime visitation upon Joseph. We might imagine that Joseph needed little convincing of what King Herod might do if he had set designs on the baby's life. Joseph did not need to be told twice to run for his life. Moses had fled Egypt once under the threat of death, but now the holy family fled to Egypt.[9]

Mary and Joseph had committed no crime nor had they engaged in civil disobedience, but Herod hunted them anyway. The powers that supposedly kept law and order threatened their very safety. Beneath the glittery façade of Herod's concern for the common welfare of his people lurked an ugly *libido dominandi*, the desire to dominate and subdue. The most expedient way to satiate that desire, as the king of Judah well knew, was brute force, coercion, and violence. In that sense, Herod was no different than any tyrant or bully in history. The fatal flaw in the will to power and the desire to dominate, as illustrated by the Bible's story, is fear. Fear fuels the desire and the will, but it also consumes what it fuels. Like gasoline, fear proves tremendously unstable and highly combustible. Fear drove Herod to hunt the child and to hunt in such an irrational manner that some scholars and skeptics doubt the stories—for what harm could a baby boy possibly do to a full grown man and king? And yet, fear of the child lashed his unbridled mind to action. Within a few short months (or perhaps even weeks), Herod himself would be dead.

The will to power confines the soul to a hamster wheel of sorts, in which the soul must go round and round faster and faster, arriving nowhere. The logic is that to gain power, one must have knowledge and control, but to have knowledge and control, one must have power over one's enemies and friends, over subordinates and colleagues. Any person who stands outside of this control, even if he be a child, presents not just a potential threat but a real violation, for that person has a modicum of power that has not been relinquished and subsumed. We must realize that the desire for power is never fully satisfied. The more power is claimed, the more it is craved. Fear reigns supreme.

The happily silent and silently happy infant Jesus presents his own alternative to Herod. The alternative of the baby is the way of simplicity, of innocence, of contentment—the alternative of childlikeness. In a world that privileges the bruising competitiveness of adulthood, God presents himself

9. Dale Allison finds nine strong parallels between Moses and the flight to Egypt. *New Moses*, 140–65.

as a baby boy. Of all the ways God could have come for our salvation, the Almighty One came as in the most helpless way. And indeed, we might say that Jesus never quite outgrew his childhood. Even as an adult he said, "Let the little children come to me" (Matt 19:14). Jesus used the example of the child to model the kingdom of heaven and to teach how every person, no matter how big or important, must enter.

The Son of the Almighty who clutched the power to disintegrate and reconstitute the world submitted himself to the free-fall helplessness of infancy. He submitted himself to the total care of others to feed him, wash him, clothe him, and love him. Though he could not speak as a babe in arms, still he taught.[10] The speechless little one remained the ever-spoken Word in the sense that the infancy of Jesus gives us the model of salvation: we must be born again, we must reenter the womb and come out as little children, as helpless babies. We must admit our need—our total and complete need, without reservation, without exception.

The way of Jesus does not offer instant gratification or intellectual prestige or political power. It is a slow way. It is an uncomfortable way. It is an inefficient way and furthermore it won't work, because, after all, it's for kids. For this reason it is laughable in the eyes of the world. But you should know that in the end laughter will save us. Upon the stage of the world we strut and stumble and act out our parts, unaware that we are in a divine comedy. Indeed, it is not a comedy because the actors make it so but because the Author wills that it not end in tragedy.

Sojourner Walk

Joseph arrived in Egypt with his young wife and newborn son. Too often we picture Joseph in our minds on stage and in costume, delivering well-rehearsed lines. We visualize him as nothing more than a minor character in a tender Christmas pageant. But there in Egypt, in the real Egypt, the place the Hebrews knew as "Mizraim," things were different. He understood neither language nor custom. He had no work or shelter to offer his family. He had never been to Egypt and couldn't Google directions or open a web page to search for apartments. There he was, head turning in every direction with the sounds of foreign tongues bouncing off his ears. No doubt he felt the pressure to provide for his family. He must have felt that it was up to him to find work, a place to stay, and the next meal.

10. Augustine, Sermo 190, *Sermons* III/6, 39.

For centuries, a significant population of Jews made their home in Alexandria, Egypt. Perhaps the holy family found refuge there among distant relatives, friends of friends, or at least compatriots and sympathetic countrymen. Somehow they survived a two-year stint in the land of sand and sun. An angel of the Lord once again appeared to Joseph in a dream and informed him that he and his family could return to the land of Israel in safety. The one who threatened the child's life was dead (Matt 2:19–20). But, just when he thought his time of wandering had come to an end, it had not. "But when he heard that Archelaus was reigning in Judea in place of his father Herod, he was afraid to go there. Having been warned in a dream, he withdrew to the district of Galilee, and he went and lived in a town called Nazareth" (Matt 2:22–23a).

Archalaeus, a son of Herod the Great, had become ruler of the regions of Judea, Samaria, and Idumea in the year 4 BC. Along with Herod Antipas and Philip I, he had inherited a share of his father's kingdom upon his death. Archelaeus had inherited the greatest portion of land—Judea, and Samaria, and Idumea, but in less than ten years' time, the Roman government removed him from power because of the outcry of complaints against him on account of his abuse of power and his mistreatment of the people.

One example will suffice. Upon the death of Herod the Great, Archelaeus had to make a trip to Rome in order to receive official sanction from the Roman emperor to rule the territory his father left for him. Before he could set sail, however, Archalaeus had to bring law and order to Jerusalem and to the Temple. The time of Passover had come and thousands of bad-tempered pilgrims funneled into Jerusalem and the Temple—Herod's Temple no less. The hated Herod was dead and the people's fury and grief over the loss of so many local heroes to Herod's sword festered and fomented. The hot crowd was in no mood to trifle. They chanted the names of Mithias and Judas, two of their own who had been wrongfully convicted and put to death by the powers. When a cohort of legionaries led by a tribune was dispatched to suppress the surly mob, the people flamed into shouts, jeers, and rock-throwing.

The skirmish was reported to Archalaeus who responded in the manner of his father: "he sent out his whole army, including the cavalry."[11] Three thousand were killed and many others wounded in the trample. Blood splattered the walls of the Temple and was left unwiped as a sign—an unforgettable sign to all Judeans.

11. Josephus, *Antiquities* 17.217, p. 473.

Archalaeus quickly earned a reputation for cruelty. Like his father, he did not hesitate to track down and kill his enemies or anyone who might threaten his rule. Joseph knew he could not go to Judea and into his sphere of influence; he could not risk Archaleaus coming after his son Jesus to finish the work that his father had begun. So Joseph and his small family bypassed Judea and settled in the far north, in Galilee. As they wound their way tediously back from Egypt and headed toward Nazareth, Joseph and Mary must have felt lost, adrift in the world, without home or help. They were sojourners, nomads, dust-footed migrants.

Luke informs us that Nazareth was the hometown of Joseph and Mary prior to the birth of Jesus (Luke 1:26, 2:39). Mark, the earliest written Gospel, confirms that Jesus came from Nazareth in Galilee and that his ministry began in Galilee (Mark 1:9, 14). Likewise John places the beginning of Jesus' ministry in Galilee (John 2:1). And this was by design from the Lord. "So was fulfilled what was said through the prophets: 'He will be called a Nazarene'" (Matt 2:23b). It had been foretold. So it would be.

But, which prophets?

Matthew says the prophets spoke of this, but there is no verse in the Hebrew Bible that matches Matthew's citation exactly, leaving modern-day commentators perplexed. Perhaps Matthew did not mean any one single prophet, but the prophets in general—he used the plural "prophets." A more satisfying solution is found in Isaiah 11:1, "A shoot will come up from the stump of Jesse; from his roots a Branch will bear fruit" where the Hebrew word for "branch" is similar to the word "Nazarene." Because the prophets sometimes spoke of a messianic "branch" or "shoot" (Jer 23:5, 33:15; Zech 3:8, 6:12), Isaiah's words in chapter 11 came to function as messianic prophecy. Indeed, the prophecy from Isaiah 11:1 played a prominent role in the rabbinic literature and Targums and in the Qumran community (1QH 6:15; 7:6, 8, 10, 19).[12] Even so, people did not automatically associate Nazareth with these messianic prophecies: "Can anything good come out of Nazareth?" (John 1:46).

We must pause to wonder what it might mean to come from Nazareth. Was it like coming from Washington, DC, or Beverly Hills, or the Hamptons? No. There was nothing fashionable or prestigious about Nazareth. Just the opposite. The prophets had foretold that the Messiah would be despised and rejected, and to be from Nazareth was by definition to be despised and rejected. Although today it is the largest city in the region, Nazareth then

12. Hagner, *Matthew 1–13*, 41.

was a forgettable dump of a farmer's town. Plopped in the northern part of Israel, it was a day's walk from the Sea of Galilee. Judeans and the cultured Jerusalem-dwellers looked down their noses at agro-towns like Nazareth that dotted the northern breadbasket of Israel. In addition to a backwaters reputation, territories like Galilee and towns like Nazareth had a history of insurrection. Harvest failures and intermittent famine put tremendous pressure on the region. The authorities squeezed the food-production capacities of the area in order to meet growing demands. Fields were picked clean and the produce hauled away, leaving the farmers and their families empty-handed and hungry. The poor Galileans felt the sting of disgruntlement and anger, but any protest or resistance only resulted in harsher treatment. Herod erected military garrisons like Sepphoris, three miles from Nazareth, to suppress labor organizers, rebels, and revolutionaries in this volatile area.

Nazareth was not a place anyone would want to be from. It was not a destination but a stopping point on the way to somewhere else. And so, we might speculate that perhaps Matthew felt obliged to explain in what sense Jesus was "a Nazarene." Did the label associate him with zealots and political revolutionaries? Was it meant as a slur on his second-class status? For Matthew it was a fulfillment of prophecy and as such it was part of salvation history. Whatever Nazareth's reputation or connotation might have been until then, it would from now on be associated with the Nazarene. The man would define the place, not the other way around.

Even so, Nazareth was an outsider town for an outsider family. Joseph, Mary, and the baby give us a family portrait of the outliers, the unremembered, the shadow people who carry history on their shoulders. What is truly surprising is that Jesus, the Son of God and savior of the world, would live his adult life in the same pattern—as a migrant, a wanderer, a nomad. Unlike so many rags-to-riches stories, Jesus did not outgrow his humble origins. He did not begin in obscurity and end in fame and fortune. He did not shed his outlier status in order to drape himself with power and royalty. In this respect he fulfilled the law of Leviticus 19:34 and Exodus 22:20, commanding the people of Israel to remember "you were aliens in the land of Mizraim"—in Egypt. He could identify with the "alien" and the blind and the demon-possessed because he remembered that he too was a poor man of poor means. He had been to Egypt as a child and he knew the stories and lessons about Egypt from the Torah.

From start to finish, Jesus remained marginalized, thwarting our expectations about how the story should go. For this reason we should pay attention to his status. Three points present themselves for inspection: a theological point, a spiritual point, and a moral point, or said differently, a lesson of faith, hope, and love.

Faith

First, a theological point. The initial point concerns our shared Christian faith, the belief that convicts and compels us. The lesson is this: the triune God of the Bible is always on mission, on the move, and so, we might say, God is by nature a migrant. It is fitting that from the beginning of his life to the end, Jesus was migratory. He could not even claim to be born in his hometown—Jesus from Nazareth was born in Bethlehem. He spent his earliest childhood in Egypt as a foreigner. Throughout his life he moved from town to town without roots, without wife, without family, without work. The one who dwelt among us had no place to dwell among us. "Foxes have dens and birds have nests, but the Son of Man has no place to lay his head" (Matt 8:20; Luke 9:58). In the end, he did not die in his hometown nor was his body buried there.

As socially unsettling as this narrative appears to those of us who cling to property, possessions, and place, the way of life that the God who is Father, Son, and Spirit has chosen is one that does not remain closed up in eternity. The triune God creates, commissions his Word, and breathes out life and energy. The Father ceaselessly sends the Son into the world on a mission of salvation. The Son forever returns to the Father's heart, returning after faithfully completing his mission, carrying with him those he has saved. The Spirit relentlessly calls and carries the power of God to the people of God on the move. The people process into the sanctuary of the church for worship, imitating the trifold God who processes into the sanctuary of time and space for us and our salvation.

At Christmas we are reminded of the eternally migratory quality of God's being. Looming over the silver froth of holiday cheer hangs an almighty weight, an electric charge to the day: the eternal God stepped onto the pages of our calendar. Every element of it is fraught with paradox: the divine one came not in bright bursts of fire but in humility, not in power and peals of thunder, but in the quietness of an unlit manger. The only one who could rightfully claim the whole world as his home found himself with no place to call his home. The Son of God clothed himself as a son of man. He met the sons and daughters of earth only to find out that they did not want to meet him; they wanted him to meet their expectations instead, and so they demanded signs and wonders.

All of this unsettles us, or at least it should. What are we to make of this "son of man"? The unworldly Nephilim spoken of in Genesis might have taken the daughters of men and had children by them, but they were unquestionably "sons of God" (Gen 6:4). The demands of Moloch and Baal in the Hebrew Scriptures might have been harsh and callous, but they were without question gods and sons of gods, and so had the right to make such demands. But what of Jesus? Where is his power, his divinity, his immunity to pain, his invincibility? With Pilate we find ourselves asking the question: If you are a king, where is your kingdom? Jesus offers no satisfying answer, only that his kingdom is not from this world, but from another place (John 18:36).

Hope

Second, a point about the spiritual life and what must we hope for. As Mary bore in her womb Jesus, so Jesus bears in his womb a kingdom that is not from this world, but from another place. It is a new kingdom with new promises. William Willimon and Stanley Hauerwas, commenting on Jesus' refusal of Satan's offer of all the kingdoms of the world, say, "Rather than running the kingdoms of the world, Jesus went about establishing a new kingdom, a kingdom in this world yet not of it."[13] The spiritual life is a life on mission. The kingdom of heaven is not a settled territory with fixed laws of order. Instead it is a way of wandering that poses as a way of living. Christians must be a people on the move. "For here we do not have an enduring city, but we are looking for the city that is to come" (Heb 13:14).

The season most reflective of this idea is the week between Christmas and New Year's. For the most part, the week keeps us plenty busy. We can do little more than clean up wrapping paper from Christmas in time to buy food and drink for New Year. And yet, the week that spans the two great celebrations presents an opportunity, if we attend to it, to look back on the holiday that has passed while looking forward to the one that approaches. And if we reflect on it at a larger level, we might say that our lives are lived

---

13. Willimon and Hauerwas, *Lord, Teach Us*, 52.

out in that time between the times, as if in the week between the two great holidays.

Christ has entered our world bearing the gift of eternal life, yet we await the fulfillment and consummation of that gift. We await the *parousia*, the "coming," the New Year's Day that will truly end the old times and begin the new. But some will say, "Where is this 'coming' he promised?" (2 Pet 3:3). This is the age-old question. Not only has every generation since Jesus' resurrection asked it, people in Jesus' own lifetime asked it of him. And even prior to his lifetime people were posing it. In answer to this question 2 Peter calls to mind Noah and the ark and the great flood. Whereas Noah's ark only saved Noah and his family and the animals, the ark of salvation must stay open as long as possible so that as many as possible—all if possible—might board and be saved. "The Lord is not slow in keeping his promise, as some understand slowness. He is patient with you, not wanting anyone to perish, but everyone to come to repentance" (2 Pet 3:9).

Love

Third, a moral point. How must we love? Now that we have seen that God is always on the move as should we be, what must we do for those around us? And not just our next-door neighbor, what about our neighbor who is not our neighbor, the sojourner in our midst, the foreigner in our community? Here we return to Mary and Joseph, who came as strangers on that cold night in Bethlehem and found, according to Luke 2:7, that "there was no room for them in the inn." In this one line from Luke we hear a weighty moral condemnation of the Bethlehemites. It's not true that there was no room. The point is that no one would make room. The inn had all of its rooms but no one would give one to a distressed mother-to-be.

We should let Martin Luther preach this point, for Luther was a man well acquainted with the necessities of a wife in labor. Although he began his career as a celibate Augustinian monk, he ended up married with six children.

> Joseph had thought, "When we get to Bethlehem, we shall be among relatives and can borrow everything." A fine idea that was! Bad enough that a young bride married only a year could not have had her baby at Nazareth in her own house instead of making all that journey of three days when heavy with child. The inn was full. No one would release a room to this pregnant woman. She had to

go to a cow stall and there bring forth the Maker of all creatures because nobody would give way. . . . Shame on you, wretched Bethlehem! The inn ought to have burned with brimstone, for even though Mary had been a beggar maid or unwed, anybody at such a time should have been glad to give her a hand.

There are many of you in this congregation who think to yourselves: "If only I had been there! How quick I would have been to help the Baby! I would have washed his linen. How happy I would have been to go with the shepherds to see the Lord lying in the manger!" Yes, you would! you say that because you know how great Christ is, but if you had been there at that time you would have done no better than the people of Bethlehem. Childish and silly thoughts are these! Why don't you do it now? You have Christ in your neighbor. You ought to serve him, for what you do to your neighbor in need you do to the Lord Christ himself.[14]

How do we find our neighbor who is not our neighbor? How do we care for the one we may not even know, have not even met? For all the political talk of illegal aliens and immigration reform, the church must find and serve real people, especially those who remain hidden from ordinary view such as migrant workers and immigrants. Just as humanity is not for the Sabbath but the Sabbath for humanity, so the church does not exist for the sake of policy but for the sake of people. Whatever the political or legal ramifications, local church congregations must be about the work of serving, protecting, and baptizing the most vulnerable among us, the strangers in our land.

For the Alien

In the first centuries of the church, a slur that was often repeated against Jesus regarded his parentage and his upbringing. Celsus, an anti-Christian Roman of the late second century, relayed the rumor in these words:

[Jesus] came from a Jewish village and from a poor country woman who earned her living by spinning. He [the person from whom Celsus learned the rumor] says that she was driven out by her husband, who was a carpenter by trade, as she was convicted of adultery. Then he says that after she had been driven out by her husband and while she was wandering about in a disgraceful way

14. Martin Luther, "Nativity," in Bainton, ed., *Martin Luther's Christmas Book*, 30–31. Also see Luther's sermon on Christmas Eve in Luther's *Sermons II*, 26.

she secretly gave birth to Jesus. And he says that because he was poor he hired himself out as a workman in Egypt, and there tried his hand at certain magical powers on which the Egyptians pride themselves; he returned full of conceit, because of these powers, and on account of them gave himself the title of God.[15]

Celsus made clear that both Mary and Jesus should be labeled as "outsiders." Mary's husband drove her out and she wandered aimlessly. Jesus hired himself out for money as a foreigner in Egypt where he learned magical arts. It would be easy to dismiss Celsus's accusations by pointing to other reliable witnesses and testimonies that contradict his account. And indeed, these slurs were not in themselves convincing but they worked because they played on people's fear of and prejudice against foreigners and nomads. The real power of the rumor lies in its appeal to our primal prejudices against drifters, outcasts, and strangers. *Jesus can't be trusted, he doesn't have a stable home life. Keep your distance, he's not from around here. He's not one of us.*

The Babylonian Talmud reported that the virgin birth story told by the Christians was a cover-up for the fact an adulterous affair produced Jesus. Mary had been wed to a man named Pandera but entered into an illicit relationship with another man named Strada (*Stada* derives from the Hebrew/Aramaic root "to go astray" or "to be unfaithful") with whom she conceived the boy. The story makes for a juicy slice of gossip, but, again, the real force of the story is how it preys upon the reader's aversion to foreigners and wanderers. Not only was Jesus the bastard child of Strada and Mary, he and his unscrupulous mother drifted from place to place until he returned to Galilee bearing "witchcraft from Egypt by means of scratches/tattoos upon his flesh."[16] In this way, the Babylonian Talmud paints a picture of Jesus slumping into town with his bag of magic tricks, covered in tattoos, smelling like a barn, and looking like a drug addict. The message is clear. Whatever might be said in favor of Jesus cannot change the verdict that he was *different*. And that should be reason enough to stay away from him.

I do not wish to linger on these old rumors about Jesus. They illustrate a simple point: we fear the "other," whoever that other, odd, out-of-place person may be. "Otherness" is not a natural state of being. It must be crafted, defined, and installed by walls of division and labels of distinction. Think of all the dividing lines we have drawn: Republican and Democrat,

15. Origen, *Contra Celsum* 1.28, p. 28–31.

16. Babylonian Talmud, tractate Shabbat 104b, in Schäfer, *Jesus in the Talmud*, 16–17.

Chinese and Korean, Israeli and Palestinian, Mexican and American, rich neighborhood and poor. Quick as lightning, we break, split, and rupture into the categories of good and bad, clean and dirty, likeable and avoidable, elect and unelect. *Disunity feels like the default setting—this is just the way things are.* Division seeps into the cracks of the church separating Roman Catholic from Kansas charismatic, white church from black church, gays from straights, women from ministry. All this is the work of sin. Sin splits us apart, dividing our will and cutting us up into little pieces of frustration. Sin binds us to decay so that "the whole creation groans as in the pains of childbirth," even up to the present time (Rom 8:22). Even our bodies "groan inwardly as we wait eagerly for our adoption as sons, the redemption of our bodies" (8:23).

What a tragic situation we find ourselves in! What a tragic situation we have created for ourselves! Who will rescue us from this body of death? Who could put back together what has been so thoroughly broken?

Thanks be to God, there is a potter who can reform broken pieces into something beautiful. There is someone who can heal the wounds of the world and rescue us from this body of death.

Jean-Marc Éla (1936–2008), the African theologian who grew up in Cameroon, endured death threats, violence, and persecution, and who died while still in exile from his homeland, had a fervent conviction that God does not remain neutral in the affairs of people. In his exposition of *My Faith as an African,* Éla declares that "the incarnation . . . establishes a form of conspiracy between God and the downtrodden."[17] The incarnation of Christ brings about the ultimate conspiracy between the Almighty Power and the powerless, between the Lord who gives blessings and those who have no blessings to spare, between heaven and hell, between Jacob and Esau (Rom 8:38). That Jesus Christ would side with the dregs of society is "the ultimate scandal of our faith."[18] The scandal should come as no surprise however, for as Éla shows, it is a scandal hidden in plain view. It is written on every page of Scripture. Éla sees Scripture as an ongoing "rereading of the exodus" in which God again and again identifies himself as "the last refuge of his beloved people subjected to exploitation, violence, and misery" (Deut 11:2–4; Prov 14:31; Isa 10:11; Amos 8:4–8).[19] Israel's prophets simply give voice to the fundamental concern of the Old Testament: that there

17. Éla, *My Faith as an African*, 105.

18. Ibid.

19. Ibid., 103.

can be no true worship without justice (Amos 4:21–4; Hosea 6:6). Faithfulness to the covenant of God requires a disavowal of all forms of brutality and oppression, not only against adult male Israelites, but especially when perpetrated against strangers and foreigners, widows and orphans, those weak and helpless (Ps 140:13; Jer 9:1–8; Neh 5:1–5; Eze 33:1–9).

A close investigation of the Hebraic Scriptures and particularly the prophets reveals a divine preoccupation often missed by those of us who have grown accustomed to freedom and legal justice: God's concern for those who get mistreated.[20] The book of Leviticus, for all of its stern instructions about the minutiae of ritual purity, displays a tender heart for foreigners and outsiders: "The alien who resides with you shall be to you as the citizen among you; you shall love the alien as yourself, for you were aliens in the land of Egypt" (Lev 19:34). This is Torah. This is Law. And in Psalm 146 we find that next to the making of heaven and earth, the psalmist praises the Lord for upholding the cause of the disempowered, giving food to the hungry, setting the prisoner free, watching over the foreigner and sustaining the fatherless and the widow (Ps 146:6–9). In the eyes of the psalmist, God's loving-kindness for the oppressed is not disconnected from God's cosmic work of creation. The making and sustaining of the physical world according to natural laws entails the making and sustaining of social justice according to moral laws.

In 2010 Shane Claiborne and Jonathan Wilson-Hartgrove composed a joint Christmastime reflection for CNN. Both of these men live out a deep commitment to the poor and marginalized in America. Jonathan Wilson-Hargrove operates the Rutba House, a family and faith-based center for community living and racial reconciliation in Durham, North Carolina. Shane Claiborne founded the Simple Way in inner city Philadelphia as a faith-based intentional community of peacemaking. In their opinion piece, they expressed a confidence that "Jesus didn't come to initiate a sentimental pause in holiday consumption" but to show the world a different way.[21] They called upon Christians to show love and concern this season to unwanted children, the millions of people who go without clean water, the 1.2 million worldwide victims of sex trafficking, the Middle Easterners who have been caught on both sides of the war on terror. Can we love even these?

---

20 Ibid., 104.

21. Shane Claiborne and Jonathan Wilson-Hartgrove, "Our Take: Rethinking Christmas," *CNN*, December 24, 2010, at http://religion.blogs.cnn.com/2010/12/24/our-take-rethinking-christmas/, accessed on June 15, 2015.

(The web-based Advent Conspiracy provides resources for individuals and churches wishing to do just that. Their creative invitation at the holiday season is to "worship fully, spend less, give more, and love all.")[22] This is the challenge of the migrant Christ.

The Jewishness of Jesus

Jesus became a refugee, uprooted by Herod and relocated to Egypt. His early childhood was marked by the experience of vagrancy that he would carry with him into adulthood. Throughout his adult ministry Jesus moved from town to town without a foxhole or nest or place to lay his head (Matt 8:20). He was the perpetual immigrant. The African American Baptist theologian Howard Thurman (1899–1981) reminds us in his book *Jesus and the Disinherited* of the plain fact that "Jesus was a Jew."[23] We so often focus on the *theological* significance of the incarnation that we tend to neglect and forget the astounding ethnic and racial significance of Jesus' Jewishness. Thurman rightly insists that Jesus' status as a Jew is not an incidental bit of trivia nor is it by accident. It is tightly wound into his work of salvation. Declining the privilege and prestige of being born Greek or Roman, he took to himself the body and personhood of a poor Jew. The Son of God "emptied himself" of power and glory (Phil 2:5–11) to the point of identifying biologically and genetically with one of the most marginalized people groups in the Greco-Roman world.

The fact of Jesus' Jewishness is easy to overlook. It occasionally gets lost amidst the pious intentions of doctrine. Historian Bill Leonard offers the example of the early Mennonites who "protected Jesus' unique DNA through the doctrine of 'celestial flesh,' by which his human and divine natures came completely from God."[24] In their attempt to preserve the sinless and divine purity of the Savior, the early Mennonite Christians denied that Jesus received anything materially or biologically from his mother, "but

---

22. Advent Conspiracy, http://www.adventconspiracy.org/, accessed December 14, 2014.

23. Thurman, *Jesus and the Disinherited*, 15. My appreciation to Curtis Freeman for this reference, *Contesting Catholicity*, 118.

24. Bill Leonard, "Advent: Jesus' DNA?," December 3, 2014, *Baptist News Global*, accessed December 3, 2014 (http://baptistnews.com/opinion/columns/item/29588-advent-jesus-dna).

passed through Mary 'like water through a tube.'"[25] In an attempt to articulate the mystery of God's holiness in Christ, they unintentionally scrubbed away other human markings, including his ethnic profile. Leonard's Mennonites provide only one example among many—Christian pastors, theologians, and ordinary believers—who so elevate Christ's unique and divine status that they detach it from his humanness, and, by consequence, from his Jewishness.

We need to be reminded of the nitty-gritty facts of Jesus' birth and bodily presence on earth. This can be done, at least in a small way, through live-action nativity displays. Francis of Assisi (1181–1226) made dramatic use of the *presepio* (Italian for "crib" or what the French call the *crèche*) one Christmas in 1224. Francis contacted a nobleman at Greccio to ask for assistance preparing a live nativity scene in the church complete with crib, hay, ox, and donkey. The "poor man from Assisi," as he was known, had devoted himself to a life of simplicity and humility in accordance with the Gospels. Surprisingly, he nonetheless displayed a remarkable flair for theatrics in communicating the faith. The Greccio congregants led the live animals into the church with lit tapers and bright torches and to the sound of music. Francis stood before the *presepio* "overcome with tenderness and filled with wondrous joy." The congregation celebrated Mass and listened as Francis, wearing deacon's vestments, preached "the birth of the poor King and the little town of Bethlehem . . . uttering the word 'Bethlehem' in the manner of a sheep bleating, he filled his mouth with the sound."[26]

Francis's live nativity reminds us that the Bethlehem stable was an actual place and that in it live animals snorted and stamped and smelled of cud. The Christ child who lay at the center was no translucent ghost, Francis would have us know, but an actual chubby-cheeked infant who cried in hunger and slept in his mother's arms.

Jacopone da Todi (1236–1306) put Francis's devotion to the manger and the Bethlehem child into warm and earthy poetry. Jacopone became a Franciscan in the generation just after Francis's death. Born in Todi, a day's walk from Assisi, he was drawn to the simple and humble way of Francis's poverty. He gave up his worldly possessions and ambitions to follow in Francis's way, which was, by extension, the way of Jesus. Jacopone proved to be a gifted poet, and this too was in keeping with the Franciscan tradition. Francis had been enamored by the songs of the troubadours and minstrels

25. Ibid.

26. Thomas of Celano, *Lives of St. Francis*, 82.

in his youth and continued to write and sing verse in his adulthood. Jacopone embraced the poetic and lyrical spirit of Francis.

In his verses about the infant Lord, Jacopone used the most heartfelt and affectionate language he could muster, describing the infant Jesus as the "Bambino," "Piccolino," "Jesulino"—the tender baby, the tiny child, the little Jesus.

> See him on the hay, that one kicking and crying,
> As if he were not a divine man.[27]

In these plain-clothed words, Jacopone expressed the absolute thoroughness of the incarnation. The divine enfleshment went beneath the surface of the skin; it stretched to the core of the Son's identity and back. The humanity of Jesus was complete in every way. No part of his person was left untouched.

Even so, Jesus of Nazareth wore his divinity lightly. You and I do not wear our humanity nearly so well. Francis and Jacopone could speak of Christ in such a rustic and domestic way only after years of disciplining their hearts and minds in the monastic way of self-renunciation. To you and me, on the other hand, the body seems weak, prone to injury and illness. It's a hotbed of desire and frustration. Deep down we wish to shuffle off this mortal coil and escape the sweating cage of blood, bone, and skin. We long to be more than we are. The theological trouble comes when we project these yearnings onto Jesus Christ. We have such a difficult time confessing the full humanity of the Lord in part because we have trouble with our own humanity. We wish to unhook our souls from our flabby flesh and get loose of our human frailties. How can we confess that God did the opposite of what we want? God wrapped himself in the very blood and skin and bone we want to remove. We have no trouble professing divinity. It's humanity we can't tolerate.

He Had No Form

If he stepped onto our streets today I suspect that we would not give Jesus a second glance. If we are honest, we would admit we are always on the lookout for Christ the King victorious, not the humble man of sorrows.

---

27. "Guardal su' l fieno, che gambetta piangente, / Como elli non fusse huomo divino." Jacopone da Todi, *Natività*, in da Todi, *Jacopone da Todi*. For translation, see Hughes and Hughes's translation, 202.

Most likely we would consciously avoid interaction with the real Jesus. To our eyes, he would never be more than a bum, a drifter, a vagabond, a sad case for the homeless shelter. Just another waste of taxpayers' money. "He had no form or majesty that we should look at him, nothing in his appearance that we should desire him" (Isa 53:2). Why would he come to earth that way? Because, as Jean-Marc Éla reminds us, "The real world of the gospel is one of hunger, wealth and injustice, sickness, rejection, slavery, and death."[28]

Throughout the 1970s and 1980s, the Latin American country of Chile boiled and steamed under the heavy lid of General Augusto Pinochet's military regime. Police intimidated, rounded up, and tortured resisters and perceived troublemakers. Many thousands simply "disappeared" (the *desaparecidos*). Fear spread its tentacles far and wide, even to the churches. In one instance, wealthy parishioners attended a Christmas Eve Mass and then called out police to disperse and arrest their fellow Christians who stood outside the church peaceably protesting torture. Ronaldo Muñoz composed a bitter and sardonic Christmas poem to commemorate the event. In part, it reads,

> And so,
> Merry Christmas!
> for oppressors and oppressed,
> for torturers and tortured.
> Because Christmas is a great mystery,
> much above such material things
> as economic oppression
> and the torture of the body.[29]

We should hear in the words of Muñoz a biting sarcasm. He derides the smug and thoughtless "Merry Christmas!" that allows for abuse, oppression, and terror. Social inequities and political injustice cannot be excused with the shrug of the shoulder and a glance toward heaven. We cannot say that because the concerns of heaven are so much higher, we should not worry about earthly concerns like oppression and torture. This is nothing more than avoidance and escapism and it has too often been the *modus operandi* of a church afraid to get its hands dirty. As Ronaldo Muñoz says

---

28. Éla, *My Faith*, 105.

29. Muñoz, "El antievangelio de algunos cristianos," quoted in Cavanaugh, *Torture and Eucharist*, 262.

elsewhere in his poem, we are only too willing to buy consensus at the cost of truth and keep the peace above all else.[30]

Salvation means adoption and redemption means being made heirs of the promise and inheritors of good things. We are pulled into the family of God and given a new identity and a new name—but you should know that it is the name of a migrant.

30. Ibid., 261.

Saints of the Season

ONE OF MY EARLIEST Christmas memories is coated with a palpable sense of anxiety. I was about six years old. The squat and square television in the living room was showing a ballet performance of the *Nutcracker*. The program, I felt, had been running too long, putting us all in danger of missing Santa Claus. If we did not all get to bed before Santa made his route over our house, I knew for sure he would skip us.

My Christmas Eve paranoia had begun the year before when, in an effort to get us monkeys to wind down for bed, my parents had said, "Santa won't stop if you're still awake. You need to go on to sleep or he'll drive on by."

Remembering that warning, I peered out the window into the black sky, searching for traces of the magical sleigh. Mom reassured me that Santa would not pass by, but how could she be certain? Santa had a lot of houses to visit. At the time, we lived in Little Rock, Arkansas, and earlier that year the tiny creek that trickled through the back of the neighborhood broke its banks and flooded everything, washing away furniture and toys. We had since moved to a newer subdivision set higher above the flood zone, but the disaster had taught me a hard lesson: tragedy could strike at any moment. I imagined Santa circling our house, realizing that the children inside were out of bed, then cracking his whip on to South America. I quick closed the curtain, scurried to my room, and put myself to bed.

As a child of Americana, I spent many Christmas Eves scanning the sky for a magical gift giver. Nearly fifty years ago, Carol Myers began searching but in a different way. She wanted her young children to know there was a person of faith behind Santa Claus. Living in Holland, Michigan, she was able to dip from the town's rich Dutch heritage to add Sinterklaas customs of setting out wooden shoes for the children on December fifth, the eve of St. Nicholas's feast day. Her two boys, Peter and Andrew, found Matchbox cars and Dutch chocolate gold coins in their shoes, and her daughter, Laura, might find barrettes along with the chocolate. St. Nicholas Day made an opportunity to talk about St. Nicholas—who he was and why he did what he did.

Myers's town of Holland boasts of having the only authentic, imported working Dutch windmill in America as well as a quaint Dutch village where sculpted candles and handmade wooden shoes can be found, along with magnets that read "Wooden Shoe Rather Be Dutch." It was here where Carol Myers found her first St. Nicholas, made of corn husk and lying in the half-price bin. She bought one for herself and for her friends who also celebrated St. Nicholas. At that time it was hard to find St. Nicholas figures, and it became almost a sport to search out new ones. Her collection grew beyond figurines to include wooden Saint Nicholas cookie molds, Saint Nicholas children's books in many languages, and Byzantine icons, all of which turned into a website dedicated to Saint Nicholas.

In 2002, her friend, Canon Jim Rosenthal, then director of communications for the Anglican Communion and author of two books on Nicholas, challenged Myers to launch a website. It is now a major site, The St. Nicholas Center, stnicholascenter.org, which contains articles on the history and person of Saint Nicholas, all kinds of resources for families, churches, and schools, including recipes for St. Nicholas cookies, descriptions of folk traditions, and links to church festivals all over the world. Receiving over a million visits each year, the site is so helpful that one time an Italian news organization lifted her account of a Nicholas festival in Italy, translated it into Italian, and posted it as their own.

After years of collecting and researching, Carol Myers learned what so many other scholars learned: the facts of Nicholas's life are few and far between. His life dates can be no more than conjectured at from circumstantial evidence. He lived between the years 260 and 333, perhaps dying as late as 343. He was born in the seaside port town of Patara, in the province of Lycia, served as bishop in the neighboring town of Myra, attended the Council of Nicaea in 325, and can be credited with a handful of deeds.

The serious historian who investigates Nicholas of Myra might grumble at the lack of reliable sources on the one hand and the abundance of hagiographic tales on the other, but he or she should keep in mind that the sources tell us what former generations took to be most important. And, while the primary sources do not record the mundane details of his life, they do indicate how people viewed Nicholas and thought of him. More than the deeds and words of Saint Nicholas, we should pay attention to the responses of people to Saint Nicholas. The legends reveal how people viewed this popular saint.

People respond to Saint Nicholas in every imaginable way. For some, Nicholas offers a good example—an illustration of virtue and devotion that all of us might follow. At the other end of the spectrum, Nicholas appears as a minor divinity—an angelic personality with a will and responsibility all of his own. The same point is true of all the Christmas saints in their wide array.

Briefly, and in no scientific manner, I will summarize the different ways believers through the ages have regarded Christmas saints. There are roughly ten ways that people have tended to view saints, and I will give special attention to Christmastime saints.

1. Everyday Christians

When the word *saint* shows up in the Bible, it refers most often to ordinary, everyday believers who are alive and in the church now. Sainthood is not so much a crown to be achieved by-and-by as it is a description of those who identify with the church as Christians (Acts 20:32). The Bible's rich usage of the term "saint" can only be appreciated by considering its etymological roots in the Greek and Hebrew of the Bible.

The English word "saint" comes from the Latin *sanctus*, but that does not do justice to the linguistic reach and flexibility of the Greek and Hebrew originals. The root word in both Greek and Hebrew refers to something or someone holy, sacred, pure, or virtuous. It can also appear in verb form and means to consecrate, hallow, make inviolable, confirm, ratify, or decree. The Hebrew word *qadesh*, plural *qadeshim*, communicates this range of meaning with the addition of a strong notion that whatever or whoever is *qadesh* has been prepared or separated out for a purpose. Religiously, something *qadesh* is set apart for God and sacrificed. In a moral context, it indicates a people set apart for God, as in Leviticus 11:44, "For I am the Lord your God. Sanctify yourselves therefore, and be holy, for I am holy." While some things might be "set apart" because they are pure and reserved for the Lord, other things might be set apart because they are impure and forbidden. So for instance, the King James Version of Deuteronomy 22:9 reads, "Thou shalt not sow thy vineyard with various seeds, lest the fruit of thy seed which thou hast sown, and the fruit of thy vineyard, be defiled." The verbal form of *qadesh* is here used to indicate what is off limits.

Hagios (ἅγιος) in the New Testament functions much like the word *qadesh*. It indicates something or someone dedicated to God, reserved for God and His service, worthy of God or perfect, sacrificial or consecrated. Appearing over 200 times in the New Testament, it can be applied to vessels, animals, and even places, such as the sanctuary (Heb 9:2). As a verb it can mean to treat with reverence or to make holy by dedication, that is, to sanctify. A fine example comes from the invocation of the Lord's Prayer that the name of the Father be "hallowed," "holy," or "revered" (ἁγιασθήτω τὸ ὄνομά σου, Matt 6:9). A curious instance of the verb form is in 1 Corinthians 7:14 in which Paul says that even unbelievers are "sanctified" in Christian marriage. Also of interest, Christ himself is referred to as a *hagios* (1 John 2:20), as are the angels, (1 Thess 3:1, and before that, Zech 14:5). Of course, *hagios* can also be applied to humans, as when Matthew 27:52 reports of tombs being opened after Christ's death on the cross, "and many bodies of the saints who had fallen asleep were raised." Paul addresses each of his letters to the "saints" or "holy ones" at Rome, Corinth, Ephesus, Philippi. The books of Acts, Hebrews, and Jude also call ordinary, everyday Christians "saints." Revelation speaks of the "saints" as those who have suffered for the name of the Lord (Rev 13:7–10, 14:12, 16:6, 17:6)

It should be evident from this quick etymological survey that "sainthood" is an all-purpose working concept in the Bible. It refers to the action of God's grace—not on the few but on the many. It can refer to the things of God and the people of God in general. In the largest sense, then, every Christian can claim the title of saint. All the baptized count as saints. When we consider the most popular and well-known Christmastime saint, Saint Nicholas, we should remember this basic point. Saint Nicholas is us. He is *saint* Nicholas with a lower case "s," redeemed in Christ the same as you, the same as me.

Saint Nicholas perfectly represents the ordinariness of Christian sainthood. When I first started researching Saint Nicholas, I was struck by the realization that here was a man who performed no electrifying miracles. He didn't preach eloquent sermons or write hefty tomes of theology. He was a saint in the way that all Christians are called to be saints—in a thoroughly quotidian way.

It was no surprise, really, that in the late nineteenth century portly and bearded men began putting on the red suit and impersonating the character of St. Nick. It was no surprise because they were impersonating someone they could call a friend and a compatriot, someone to whom they could relate. In the early twentieth century, schools for training and certifying Santas began popping up in various parts of the country and proving that the spirit—not the body or the intellect or the holiness of St. Nick—was what counted. Charles W. Howard waved to the crowds as Santa Claus in the Macy's Thanksgiving Day parade for nearly twenty years. He opened a famous Santa Claus School in Albion, New York in 1937, where hundreds of Santa would-be's earned BSC degrees (Bachelor of Santa Claus). In addition to "proper dress and use of make-up" and "live reindeer habits," students would be introduced to the "Do's and Don'ts of Santa Clauses."

> Be Jolly
> Be Firm
> Be Clean
> Be Impartial
> Don't Fall Asleep While on the Job
> Don't promise children something they might not get
> Don't drink, smoke or chew on the job
> Don't accept money from a parent in front of a child[1]

This condensed list represents a few of the expectations put upon any respectable representative of the North Pole. Anyone who could master these traits had the makings of a genuine Claus. "Love your God, your Church, and your Neighbors. Be kind to the little children. Be generous to the poor. Be helpful, respectful and show consideration to the aged and the needy."[2] These morals and maxims apply not just to Santas in training; they apply to all the saints. The best attributes of Santa Clauses are really no more than the basic duties of all good Christians—to listen well and treat children with gentleness and respect, be quick to chuckle and slow to anger, give gifts and spread kindness to everyone you meet.

---

1. *It's Fun to be a Real Santa Claus*, 11.
2. Ibid., 12.

2. Models/Exemplars

Ephesians 2:19 encourages the community of believers to act like "fellow citizens with the saints and members of the household of God." God calls all of us to act like saints, but in truth, few do. And so, the title "saint" often gets reserved for certain individuals—those who demonstrate devotion to the gospel most clearly and dramatically. Saint Paul advised his churches to "follow my example, as I follow the example of Christ" (1 Cor 11:1; Phil 3:17; 2 Thess 3:7–9). Saints are models and examples for the rest of us to imitate.

The Southern Baptists, that clan of Christianity not known for venerating the saints, revere the name Lottie Moon at Christmastime because they see in her a model and exemplar of true discipleship. Her life story has had a profound impact on the evangelistic zeal and missionizing spirit of the Baptists. Her example has spurred many men and women to serve abroad. Lottie Moon (1840–1912) answered the call to "go out among the millions," venturing deep into the Chinese countryside to share of her faith, her resources, and her soul.

A few days before Christmas in 1858, the young Lottie Moon was converted to the Gospel of Jesus Christ and baptized. It happened in this way. The First Baptist Church in Charlottesville held a series of inquiry meetings and Moon decided to attend one. Her cousin recounted, "[Lottie said] she was going to church that night to see what that old fool had to say and came back converted."[3] The experience set her on a trajectory to China. From that moment on, she felt a growing sense of urgency to do something bold for Christ, and eventually "answered the call" of the mission field, struck out for "foreign parts," and landed at a Baptist outpost in China.

In 1887, after living in China for fourteen years, she floated the idea of establishing the week before Christmas as a time for giving to foreign missions. Money had always been tight on the mission field and added to that, it had proven difficult to raise back in the States. She pleaded her case in this way: "Is not the festive season when families and friends exchange gifts in memory of The Gift laid on the altar of the world for the redemption of the human race, the most appropriate time to consecrate a portion from abounding riches and scant poverty to send forth the good tidings of great joy into all the earth?"[4] Her cry for help deeply affected Annie Armstrong,

3. Quoted in Sullivan, *Lottie Moon*, 25.

4. Lottie Moon, Letter from Sept. 15, 1887, Tungchow, *Foreign Mission Journal*

Fannie Heck, and others, resulting in the creation of what would come to be known as the Lottie Moon Christmas Offering in 1888 and in the same year, the Woman's Missionary Union, a multistate, female-led organization to oversee the collection of the offering. To this day, her name and legacy continues to be connected with the week of Christmas in the annual offering campaign.

Before taking leave of Moon, we should note that her story would intersect one more time with Christmas. She died on Christmas Eve, 1912, at the age of 72.

In addition to the example of Lottie Moon, we again return to Saint Nicholas of Myra. Here is one story from his life that exemplifies his courageous and noble behavior and can serve as a model for the rest of us. During a particularly severe famine in the region of Lycia and the town of Myra, Nicholas, so it is said, procured grain from a passing supply ship. This was no small feat on account of the fact that the grain ship carried the sacred *annona*, the annual imperial grain supply. Bound for the emperor who waited for it in Constantinople, the grain ship would be permitted under no condition to sell any of its freight. The annual arrival of grain ships from Alexandria was greeted in Constantinople with solemn procession. The Emperor led a train of dignitaries to watch the gain being deposited in heaping mounds at the great Imperial Granary known simply as *Lamia*—"Jaws."[5] Even so, by the power of Providence, the bishop Nicholas convinced the master of the ship to save the town and release a portion of his grain. Legend later added a miraculous conclusion to the tale. When the ship's captain protested that the cargo was not for sale, saying that it had been weighed and measured in Alexandria, Nicholas encouraged him to have faith in God. Nicholas dispersed the grain to the grateful people who found they now had enough to save some for planting the next season. Miraculously, when the ship captain arrived in Constantinople, his vessel was found to contain exactly the same amount of grain that had been loaded in Alexandria.[6] The Lord had provided both for the people of Myra and for the courageous and trusting ship captain.

The story ranks as one of Carol Myers's favorites not because of its miraculous conclusion, but because of its humane nobility. Nicholas, who was not a politician or man of business, showed broad concern for people

---

(December 1887). Quoted in Harper, ed., *Send the Light*, 224.

5. Brown, *Through the Eye of a Needle*, 14.

6. English, *Saint Who Would Be Santa Claus*, 155–56.

in need—and not just the members of his own family or his own congregation of Christian believers, but the whole city. Myers takes this story as encouragement for families, small groups, and churches to celebrate Saint Nicholas Day by giving back. "The true spirit of Saint Nicholas is helping people in need," she said. "Churches might do a clothing drive or a toy drive, or provide service at a food bank."

3. Teachers

We have looked at saints as ordinary believers and as examples to follow. But the value of saints such as Augustine, Gregory of Nazianzus, Catherine of Siena, and Hildegard von Bingen, is directly linked to the beauty and wisdom of their teachings and writings. Some saints wrestled with the deepest mysteries of the faith and resolved some of its most pressing dilemmas. They are called saints because they are teachers.

It must be quickly added, however, that Christmas, far from being a time of rigorous scholastic work, is generally associated with holiday reprieve from the drudgeries of school. Public school students delight in a two- to three-week break from classes. The indulgence in a break from schoolwork at this time of year is no modern invention but a time-honored tradition. In olden times, Saint Thomas's Day, December 21, elicited wild frivolity and misbehavior and "barring out the master." Children in England, Denmark, and elsewhere locked their teachers out of the schoolhouse or even bound them to their chairs and then forced them to buy back their freedom or negotiate entry into the building, usually with ale or punch or cakes. In Austria, Wesphalia, and Holland, the day was associated with sleeping in late, possibly because it was often the shortest day of the year with the longest stretch of dark night. The last one out of bed or to the table or to school received good-natured ridicule as "lazybones" or *Domesesel* ("Thomas ass").[7]

We return to Saint Nicholas, who was no teaching saint, but whose name is associated with the midwinter academic break. He did not pen any important theological tracts nor did he lecture on the complexities of the faith. He attended the theologically charged and historically decisive Council of Nicaea in 325, which first produced the Nicene Creed, but there is no indication that he played a significant role in the proceedings. In the late fourteenth century the rumor began to circulate that Nicholas had jumped

7. Miles, *Christmas in Ritual and Tradition*, 224–25.

up during one of the council's sessions and slapped an Arian heretic in the face out of righteous indignation. Although it makes for entertaining drama, such a legend does nothing to elevate Nicholas's reputation as an academic.

Despite the fact that he was no serious scholar, Nicholas's name and patronage is connected with students, owing to a popular medieval drama that tells of three seminarians or theology students who spent the night at an inn only to be butchered by the proprietors. The bodies were disposed of, but Saint Nicholas came to the rescue and restored them to life. Another legend appended to various medieval retellings of the "Life of Saint Nicholas" relates of an instance when Nicholas acted the part of the teacher giving instruction in a most memorable way.

The tale to which I am referring is set in a drafty and drab eleventh-century monastery of the Cluniac order. A notable composer, Reginold, had recently completed a new anthem praising God and celebrating the works of Saint Nicholas. The piece circulated about but the prior of the monastery, who was very strict about such things, would not permit his Cluniac monks to sing it. The monks were disappointed but submitted to the decision.

> But when the prior lay down on his cot as did the others, lo, the blessed Nicholas appeared visibly before him with a fearful demeanor and upbraided him in the bitterest terms for his obstinacy and pride. Dragging him from bed by the hair, he shoved him to the floor of the dormitory. Beginning with the anthem *O pastor aeterne*, and with each modulation inflicting most severe blows on the back of the sufferer with the switches which he held in his hand, he taught the wayward prior to sing the whole from beginning to end.[8]

The thought of Nicholas thrashing a recalcitrant prior until he had "learned his lesson" dramatically contrasts the standard American image of Santa Claus as a kindly old grandfather who wears a perpetual smile. Who knew he had it in him?

In medieval and early modern minds, the presence of a switch or whip in the hand of Nicholas did not necessarily indicate that he was mean or angry or sadistic. It was primarily to identify him as a teacher. Teachers in the pre-twentieth century world were popularly viewed as authoritarian disciplinarians. Switches, rods, and whips were commonly associated with

---

8. *Cat. Cod. Hag. Paris.* I, 510–511, translated by Jones in *St. Nicholas Liturgy*, 47–49.

schoolteachers and classrooms in the imaginations and storytelling of the medieval and early modern eras. Echoes of this identification can still be seen in the tradition of Santa Claus quizzing children about their behavior and making a list of naughty and nice.

In Germany today, someone dressed as Bishop Nicholas will come to the house with a ledger and ask children whether they have behaved and whether they had done their homework and helped their parents. In pious European homes children may even prepare Bible verses or catechetical answers to recite to the Christmastime bishop. Even in the States where the expectations are much looser, parents still threaten—albeit tongue-in-cheek—to put a lump of coal in the stockings of misbehaving children.

Shades of Nicholas the teacher continue to appear to this day in his roles as inspector of virtue, protector of children, and bearer of the cane, switch, and whip. His authority as bishop, his gentleness as Father Christmas, his sternness as evaluator of behavior, and his generosity as distributor of rewards and gifts make for a warmly paletted picture of a teacher saint.

4. Witnesses to God's power and steadfastness

Saints show us what God can do and has done in the lives of individuals. Saints are special not only because of what they have done but because of what God has done in and through them. The saints are embodiments of God's grace, provision, protection, and faithfulness. They testify to "the riches of [Christ's] glorious inheritance in the saints" and to the transformative power of God's Spirit (Eph 1:18). The martyrs, those who have died for their convictions, such as Stephen, Polycarp, Perpetua, Maria Goretti, Martin Luther King Jr., and Oscar Romero, witness to the divine peace that is given in the midst of crisis and despair.

The day following December 25, that is to say the second day of Christmas, December 26, the church calendar remembers Saint Stephen. Although Stephen was not one of the original twelve disciples, he received the daunting honor of being the first martyr of the faith. He watched the heavens part their curtains as his lifeblood trickled out of his body. As members of an angry Jerusalem Sanhedrin stoned him to death, he saw the Son stand at the right hand of the Father (Acts 7:55). Stephen died because of the name of Jesus Christ.

As important as his martyrdom is to Christian history, his final words are perhaps of even greater significance. He said, "Lord, do not hold this sin against them" (Acts 7:60). With his last breath he articulated the first law of Christian ethics: forgiveness. His words represent no more and no less than the words of Jesus on the cross, "Forgive them Father for they know not what they do." Pronounced by Jesus, they carry the weight of a divine verdict: the Father will forgive any and all who fall under the shadow of the cross of Christ. Spoken by Stephen at the hour of death they become something else; they become a prescription and an imperative. On the lips of Stephen they are transformed into a mandate for the Christian life. And so, on the day after Christmas, when we are tempted to contemplate nothing greater than leftovers and trash bags full of wrapping paper, the church calendar would have us think on Stephen, the cost of discipleship, and the first principle of Christian action: forgive them.

The third day of Christmas, December 27, commemorates Saint John, the apostle and evangelist who understood that the quiet baby wrapped snuggly in the manger was the way, the truth, and the life (John 14:6). The fourth day of Christmas, December 28, solemnly observes the Holy Innocents, the boys of Bethlehem slain on Herod's order. In the Latin calendar, the feast falls on the twenty-eighth of December. Although Saint Stephen's Day comes before the Innocents' in the calendar, the Innocents predate Stephen. The children did not die in the name of Christ but in his stead. And so, even though Stephen is remembered as the first martyr, the young ones were the first to lose their lives. For the Holy Innocents we can only weep. This is the world into which our Savior was born, a world that does not hesitate to dispose of the most vulnerable and precious ones among us.

The witness of the martyrs reminds us that our personal survival is not the highest calling or the final promise of the gospel. Naturally, everyone wants to live a full life to a ripe old age and die in peace and security. The record of history shows that many are not granted this desire. Those who follow the one who told his followers to carry their cross must understand that the cross is a constant reminder of death. Jesus made clear to his followers that they must ready themselves to die and to lay down their lives for their friends. Death should never be glorified or sought out. It is not a good thing, nor should it be spoken of lightly or flippantly. The sober teaching of the gospel, however, is that there are things worth dying for.

And we must remember that in Christ, death is not the end of life.

5. The cloud of witnesses

Hebrews 12:1 describes the community of believers as "surrounded by such a great cloud of witnesses." Believers who die do not cease to exist. They stand before God in worship (Rev 7:9–17, 8:4). The Church with a capital "C" extends beyond whoever happens to be alive at this moment. Death does not terminate membership. The Church consists of the living and the dead; it is the eternal people of God. This is the Church "catholic" with a lowercase "c"—not the Roman Catholic Church only, but catholic in the sense of ecumenical, universal, and whole.[9] All Christians who make up the worldwide people of God can find lodging within this house of many rooms. Saints remind us that the body of Christ is much larger than any individual, local church, or denomination (Heb 2:11, 10:10). Remembering the saints who came before us reminds us of our long and lovely heritage that stretches backwards in time and outwards around the globe.

There are many moments in the Advent calendar to remember, recognize, and relish in the great "cloud of witnesses." For example, the church dedicates the second Sunday before Christmas to the holy forefathers and mothers—the ancestors of Christ according to the flesh, beginning with Adam, Abraham, Sarah, David, and ending with Zechariah and John the Baptizer—and the Sunday immediately before Christmas to all the holy fathers and mothers who lived in obedience to God before the advent of God's Son. Special emphasis is given in the Orthodox communion to Daniel and his friends who refused to worship a graven image, even at the risk of their own lives:

> Great are the accomplishments of faith,
> for the Three Holy Youths rejoiced in the flames as though at the
> waters of rest,
> and the prophet Daniel appeared
> a shepherd to the lions as though they were sheep[10]

Thomas Becket is remembered during this season along with Basil and Gregory of Nazianzus, two of the great Cappadocian Fathers whose

---

9. The term *catholic* is certainly a contested term, but it is a term worth preserving because it is a historic term whose usage dates back to the very earliest conversations about the church. The term is not the exclusive property of the Roman Catholic Church. It can describe "a quality in congregations of being whole, typical, or ordinary" and "the sense of catholicity shared by all Christian churches." Freeman, *Contesting Catholicity*, 254–55. Also see McClendon and Yoder, "Christian Identity in Ecumenical Perspective," 562–78.

10. *Book of Divine Prayers and Services*, 366.

theological texts are consulted to this day and who are venerated as two of the three Doctors of the Eastern Orthodox Church. Dozens of other saints make appearances from the cloud of witnesses during the Advent season, including the biblical prophets Nahum, Habakkuk, and Hannah as well as nonbiblical heroes and heroines of the faith like Barbara, Ambrose, Daniel the Stylite, Ignatius of Antioch, Anastasia of Rome, John of the Cross, and the Polish princess Kunigunde. Two luminaries of the twentieth century, the Swiss Reformed theologian Karl Barth and the Trappist mystic Thomas Merton both died on December 10, 1968. And so we might remember them as December saints too. Countless other names might be added to the roster—friends, family, mentors, pastors, priests, and teachers who have some connection with the Christmas season.

The Italian Franciscan theologian Bonaventure (1221–1274) once envisioned the birth of Christ as an occasion for an extravagant banquet to which countless saints have been invited: "On great feasts it is the custom to invite other people to the banquet, and if this is done to show charity, it is praiseworthy. Christ, therefore, did not want to be on His own at the banquet of joy, and so He invited His companions, friends, and servants to share in the joy."[11] Bonaventure, in true Italian style, pictures Christmas as a social get-together, *una festa*, a jamboree, a wing-ding, a party for friends. A great number of classical antiphons sung at the Vesper services leading up to Christmas Eve begin with a full-chested vocal heave—O!—"O Wisdom," "O Root of Jesse," "O Dayspring," "O King of the Nations," "O Emmanuel."[12] Why? I can't say for sure, but one reason might be that the season invites singing and singing invites company. The saints of Advent crowd the manger with song and laughter and presents and cake. Who wouldn't want to join this hee-haw hootenanny?

6. Face of God to us

On the traditional church calendar, we find so many saints' feasts clustered around the stable. It is as if the one star perched over Bethlehem's stall has attracted the lights of thousands of other stars in the heavens. Thinking about saints provides believers with a way to understand Christianity and relate to a sometimes mysterious God. Saints give a human face to the

11. Bonaventure, *De sancto Stephano, sermo* 1; Q IX: 478b–c. Quoted in Saward, *Cradle*, 31.

12. Miles made this observation in *Christmas in Ritual and Tradition*, 92.

supernatural. They are approachable in ways that God is not, or at least in ways that God does not seem to be to many individuals. The Christian revolution in religion consists in the confession that God is now approachable through Christ. Through Christ, the Creator and Judge of heaven and earth desires relationship with each of us. Even so, our hearts are weak and we need the saints to witness God's new relationship with us and for us.

In 2002, Pope John Paul II canonized Juan Diego Cuauhtlatoatzin (1474–1548), the first saint indigenous to the Americas. It is hard to overestimate the importance of Juan Diego for the Latino and especially Mexican sense of religious identity. On the ninth of December, 1531, the humble Indian peasant named Juan Diego trudged along the dirt path listening to the breeze flicker over the rocks and stubble when he heard the voice of Mother Mary, the Virgin. She spoke in his native language of Nahuatl. She instructed him to build a church on the Tepeyac Hill, on the north end of today's Mexico City. Juan Diego did the most sensible thing he could think to do. He confided to his bishop. The bishop cautiously asked for some evidence of the supposed encounter.

On the hill of Tepeyac, on December 12, Mother Mary arranged flowers on Juan Diego's *tilma*, his thin cloak made of cactus fibers. Popular piety believes that Saint Luke, the Gospel writer who had personal contact with Jesus' mother, drew a portrait during his lifetime that closely resembled what Juan Diego Cuauhtlatoatzin saw. The over-awed peasant immediately showed the image to his bishop. When he did, the flowers fell away. Miraculously, the imprint of the Virgin remained on the *tilma*, which can be inspected to this day at the Basilica of Our Lady of Guadalupe. A moving walkway transports the millions of annual visitors and pilgrims past the icon for viewing. A poignant quotation from the rector of the basilica, Diego Monroy Ponce, frames the story's connection to Christmas, "Christmas here is the 12th of December because that's the day Our Lady gave birth to this continent."[13]

Like Juan Diego and Our Lady of Guadalupe, Saint Nicholas has also been the face of God to countless people around the world. In 1383, so one Russian story goes, a peasant folding his way through wooded hills one evening noticed a faint and flickering light near the banks of the Velikaya River. The man, Semyon Agalakov by name, veered off his trail and found the light source to be an abandoned Icon of Saint Nicholas, an image of

13. "Christmas Comes Early in Latin America," *The Canadian Press*, December 3, 2010, http://search.proquest.com/printviewfile?accountid=9858.

the saint painted on a flat wood panel. He picked it up and carried it to his humble log cabin dwelling to keep it safe, but the icon was not content to be tucked away and unknown. Soon miracles began to attach themselves to the icon and pilgrims from far and wide sought out the wonder. To this day, as many as 40,000 pilgrims make the 105-mile trek in June from Kirov to Velikoretsky. Most are on foot though some ride in buses. The icon, for all else that it symbolizes, represents a simple, rustic, and familiar face of God to the people of the region.

Let me pause for a personal reflection. I grew up in a wonderful, loving family. My parents did their best to rear us in the most biblical way. We attended an evangelical, culturally conservative, "Spirit-filled" church. The Christianity of my childhood taught that the things of this world could not be trusted. Batman wore a mask with horns and the Smurfs were demonic for reasons too numerous to count. Television served as Satan's box of temptation and mind control. Halloween was his holiday. Our guiding principle could be stated simply: to be "in the world but not of it." Even seemingly Christian holidays like Easter should be approached with caution. Celebrating Jesus' resurrection was fine, but as for the bunny and the eggs, well . . . the devil finds ingenious ways to infiltrate.

When it came to Christmas, my parents found themselves at a loss. They wanted us kids to sing carols, hang stockings, string lights, and find presents under a tree on Christmas morning. We watched *The Grinch Who Stole Christmas* and the Charlie Brown specials on TV. But, they also felt convicted by the "true meaning" of Christmas—our Savior's birth. For this reason, Santa Claus was never viewed as a fellow worker in the vineyard of the Lord.

Santa was secular; at best he represented the commercialized greed of the season, at worst he was the pied piper of paganism luring children away from the true meaning of Christmas with his sack of goodies. Even as my parents opened the flue to grant him access to our chimney on the twenty-fourth, they reiterated that Jesus, not some elf from the North Pole, was the reason for the season.

It would take me years to learn that Jesus Christ and Santa Claus don't have to be foes; they are friends committed to the same truth. Who knows? Saint Nicholas, and perhaps even Santa Claus, might be the only face of God some people will ever see or pay attention to. For that reason alone people of faith should care about Saint Nicholas and Santa Claus. In so doing, they might find the face of God in faces once overlooked.

7. Patron of people groups, professions, and places

Patrons fall somewhere between spiritual protectors and group mascots. Think of the young girls dressed in white and carrying candles, tapers, and torches on Saint Lucy's Day throughout Sweden. The commemoration of Saint Lucy falls on the thirteenth of December. Saint Lucy, also known as Saint Lucia of Syracuse, is depicted in Christian art holding a saucer containing two eyeballs. According to one legend she tore out her own eyes when forced into an arranged marriage. According to another her eyes were dug out by pagan persecutors. Not surprisingly, she is the patron saint of people with poor eyesight.

Saint Nicholas, in addition to being the patron saint of Christmas, has also acquired the patronage of nearly fifty different people groups, including apothecaries, orphans, button makers, florists, haberdashers, judges, newlyweds, old maids, pirates, children, pawnbrokers, thieves, and travelers, to name but a few. In Pollutri, traditional Italians light fires under cauldrons to cook *fave* beans on December 6 in honor of Nicholas as the patron of poor shepherds. In 2013 the Patriarch of Moscow consecrated a floating lighthouse to Saint Nicholas, the patron saint of boatmen and all who traverse open waters. The lighthouse displays eight Nicholas-related icons and sits at the confluence of Russia's Irtysh and Ob rivers. Sociologically speaking, what is the function of Nicholas for those Russian rivermen whose vessels slip past his image on their voyage downstream? It seems to be one of patron.

Artists have historically pictured Nicholas with three children in a barrel based on a popular medieval legend in which Nicholas resurrected three children who had been butchered and crammed into a pickling barrel. The tale is as bizarre as it is grisly. But it proved enormously popular amongst ordinary folk and was presented time and again on stained glass, wood panels, tapestry, and frescoed surfaces. For hundreds of years artists, bookbinders, and engravers reproduced the scene and eventually began to depict it in shorthand. It became standard to picture Nicholas with three children coming out of a barrel. The barrel and the three naked children at the feet of Nicholas helped to identify him and to recall the popular story.

Over time people either forgot or never learned the suspenseful and dramatic tale of the barrel and the children. One can imagine a mother standing before an old wooden placard depicting the saint in bishop's robes and a barrel of three naked children. Bamboozled, she furrows her brow and tries her best to offer some reasonable explanation to her own inquisitive children who ask her questions about the picture. What is clear to her and to so many others is Nicholas's patronage of children. He must be a patron saint of children because children always appear in the frame with him. The mother might console her young ones with this information and tell them that's all they need to know.

Brewers noticed something besides the children. They noticed the barrel and came to believe that Nicholas must be their patron saint as well because he always appeared with a wooden barrel.

The Basilica di San Nicola in Carcere in Rome, Italy, provides another example of how patronages evolve. The church was constructed over the location of an old municipal prison, hence the name it came to be called by: "Saint Nicholas in Chains," San Nicola in Carcere. Although the name had nothing to do with Nicholas in chains, the temptation to invent an association between Nicholas and the prison beneath the foundations of the basilica—which has been excavated and can be visited by tourists—proved irresistible. Tales quickly accumulated of Nicholas languishing in that very prison, of mothers praying to Nicholas for the release of their sons from incarceration, and repentant criminals making votive offerings at the church. Not surprisingly, Nicholas eventually became the patron saint of prisoners and those falsely accused.

8. Intermediaries

Saints serve as go-betweens and intercessors before the Almighty Maker of heaven and earth. In a truly dire situation, such as a child on her death bed, a parent might invoke the name of Saint Jude who specializes in hopeless causes. When prayed to in this way, Saint Jude acts in this way as an intermediary, taking an urgent request to the heart of God. In the same way that close friends or family members might ask each other to pray to the Lord on their behalf, so Christians might ask for the prayers of those faithful believers who have already passed from this life. "The prayers of the saints" are as "golden bowls full of incense" in the nostrils of God (Rev 5:8). According to the official *Catechism of the Catholic Church*, those who dwell in heaven "do not cease to intercede with the Father for us" and "by their fraternal concern is our weakness greatly helped."[14] Saint Nicholas often functions for many Christians as an intermediary between heavenly

---

14. *Catechism of the Catholic Church*, Part 1, Section 2, Chapter 3, Article 9, Paragraph 5.

power and earthly hopes. The Troparion for December 6[15] in the Byzantine liturgy observes Nicholas's "greatness through humility and wealth through poverty" and asks that he "intercede with Christ our God to save our souls."[16] The prayer requests Nicholas to plead with God on our behalf.

In the history of ideas, Anselm the archbishop of Canterbury (1033–1109) embodied the essence of medieval scholasticism. He wrote rigorously argued tracts of theology and thick treatises of advanced philosophy. Most famously, for instance, he proved the existence of God on the basis of pure reason. What is regularly forgotten is that he was not always the archbishop of Canterbury. For thirty-four years, Anselm trained himself in the ways of mystical prayer and deep meditation at the monastery at Bec, in the territory of Normandy, France. This was a man of deep faith as well as sweeping philosophical intellect. In a prayer he once wrote to Saint Nicholas, he pondered the meaning of saints as advocates and intermediaries on behalf of earthly petitioners. Speaking directly to Nicholas, Anselm asks,

> Why, sir, are you called upon by all men in all the world unless you
> are to be the advocate of all who pray to you?
> Why does this sound in all ears,
> "My lord, St Nicholas," "My lord, St Nicholas,"
> unless it means,
> "My advocate, St Nicholas," "My advocate, St Nicholas"?[17]

As Anselm articulates it, those who call upon saints in prayer are calling upon advocates and intercessors before God. No saintly advocate has been more beloved and more often called upon by people in distress than Mary, the mother of our Lord.

Two days in particular during the Christmas season have been reserved for her: December 8 and January 1. Roman Catholics reverently commemorate the immaculate conception of Mary on December 8, the moment when Mary was conceived with grace and without the taint of sin in the womb of her mother, Anne. Over the years, at least since the seventh century, January 1 has been associated with Mary as well. Roman Catholics observe it as a Marian day of high importance. In fact, in 1974 Pope Paul

---

15. It should be noted that December 6 in the Gregorian calendar (the one used by the United States and much of the world) is November 23 in the Julian calendar (still in use in the liturgical East) while December 6 in the Julian is December 19 in the Gregorian.

16. *Divine Liturgies*, 274.

17. Anselm, *Prayers and Meditations of St. Anselm*, 186.

IV officially designated January 1 as the "Solemnity of Mary, Mother of God." In the process he may have inadvertently downgraded the feast for the circumcision of Jesus, also celebrated on the first of January, the eighth day after his birth.

The connection between Mary and New Year's Day comes from a richly symbolic reading of Scripture. Christ's birth, theologically speaking, marks "the birthday of the whole human race."[18] With the Advent of Christ the human race starts over. We are reborn in Christ. On New Year's Day we are reminded of the gift of the new Eve, the mother of a new humanity through Jesus Christ. Christ's birth is not a season as much as it is the dawn of a new era and a new history. The comparison of Eve to Mary and Mary to Eve is an ancient one and can be traced back to the writings of such early theologians as Justin Martyr, Irenaeus, Tertullian, and Epiphanius, among others. Hildegard von Bingen (1098–1179), the twelfth-century Sybil of the Rhine, won great renown for her highly original revelations, visions, letters, and hymns. In one such sequence on the Virgin, Hildegard contrasts Eve, the "strong rib of Adam," with Mary, "beloved beyond measure."[19] Eve's sin of disobedience in the garden is compared to the shock and sorrow of a miscarriage. "With ignorant hands she plucked at her womb and bore woe without bounds." Mary's obedience, by contrast, marks the joyous moment of salvation's birth. The birth of Christ looked to Hildegard like a sunrise whose rays "burnt the whole of [Eve's] guilt away."[20] What had been lost in the garden so long ago was won back and more in the new life that entered the world through Mary.

9. Divine agents

The Gospel according to Mark reports that Jesus gave his disciples "power over unclean spirits . . . and they went out . . . and cast out many devils, and anointed with oil many that were sick, and healed them" (6:7–13). Jesus added, in the Gospel of John, "Truly, truly, I say to you, he who believes in me will also do the works that I do; and greater works than these will he do" (John 14:12). Should we take these words at face value? The apostles and saints in heaven have power over unclean spirits and illness and are

18. Basil, *Homily 27*, *Patrologia Graeca* 31:1473A. Also see Gregory of Nazianzen, *Oratio* 38.4, *Patrologia Graeca* 36:316B.

19. Hildegard von Bingen, "O virga ac diadema," in *Symphonia*, 129.

20. Ibid., 131.

commissioned to perform works on earth. The saints are God's ambassadors, God's agents, God's messengers, God's helpers on earth. Does this mean, for instance, that one might call upon Saint Anthony of Padua when searching for a missing item? As the jingle goes, "Saint Anthony, please look around; something is lost and must be found."

A man and his wife and their baby from Kiev made a pilgrimage on a boat up the Dneper River to Vyshgorod to celebrate the feast day of two very important Russian saints, Boris and Gleb, on July 24. After paying their respects, the devout family sailed homeward when tragedy struck. Lulled by the gentle rocking of the boat, the mother nodded off and her baby slipped from her arms and into the river. The child sank and drowned. The parents were crushed with grief and cried, not to Saints Boris and Gleb, but to Nicholas, whom they called the Wonderworker, "O Holy Wonderworker Saint Nicholas, you are the swift deliverer of all in distress, perform a miracle and save an innocent child from death."[21]

In the still darkness of the night, Saint Nicholas slipped out of heaven and into the river where he retrieved the child's body. Taking it to the Saint Sophia Cathedral in Kiev, he laid it before his own icon. Early the following morning, a sacristan of the cathedral heard the sounds of a baby crying inside the sanctuary. He took the sounds to be evidence not of a miracle, but of the ineptitude of the cathedral's guard, who must have let a vagrant mother and her child slip past his notice. The guard protested and showed the angry sacristan the locked doors. No one had entered. The two men went inside and found a child, still wet from the river, alive in front of Saint Nicholas's icon. Not knowing whose child it was, they informed the Metropolitan, who instructed them to go to the market, make an announcement, and try to find the baby's parents.

Among the many pious and curious people who came to the Kiev cathedral to see the wondrous sight was the father of the dead child. Terrified and amazed, he said nothing to anyone but ran home to his wife. The two reclaimed their lost child and gave praise to God and thanks to God's agent, Nicholas.

In this story, Nicholas acted as a divine agent. More often, angels perform that role. Angels are numbered among the saints in the sense that they are messengers of God and agents of his will. September 29 celebrates Saint

---

21. Carol Myers, St. Nicholas Center, citing Boguslawski, *The Vitae of St. Nicholas*, vol. 2, 87–88. http://www.stnicholascenter.org/pages/lost-and-found/, accessed on December 19, 2014.

Michael, Saint Raphael, and Saint Gabriel. Though they are angelic beings they wear the label "saint." They are holy ones. Saint Gabriel has special significance for the nativity. His Hebrew name means "God is my strength" and he appears twice in the book of Daniel, but more importantly for our purposes, he appears twice in Luke's nativity story. He delivers instructions, announcements, and explanations from the throne of heaven.

Not only does Gabriel play a pivotal part in Jesus' birth, he also makes star appearances in Judaism and Islam. The Qur'an refers to him by the Arabic name Jibril. In the important *Hadith of Gabriel*, the angel Gabriel/ Jibril interrogates Muhammad about faith, submission to God, and perfection, the basic tenets of Imam, Islam, and Ihsan. The prophet Muhammad satisfies Gabriel's queries by vocalizing the core of the Muslim faith—the five pillars and the six articles (Sahih Bukhari 1.2.48). Within Judaism, Gabriel plays a part in the early Jewish book of 1 Enoch. In that text he functions less as a messenger and more as a destroyer of enemies and protector of friends (1 Enoch 10:9; 20:7). Perhaps for this reason, rabbinic literature tended to identify him as the otherwise unnamed angel of Jerusalem's destruction mentioned in Ezekiel. Because of his many roles in many different dramas, religious art depicts Gabriel holding a trumpet, a horn, a branch from Eden's paradise, a lantern, a lily, or a scroll. He has proven over the course of time to be more than a winged "extra" in the annual Christmas pageant, but a true agent of God's will.

10. Minor divinities

At the farthest end of the spectrum, saints function as substitute deities, additional divinities, or supernatural forces to be reckoned with on their own. Saint Nicholas sometimes functions in this way. With this understanding in mind, the folklore scholar Phyllis Siefker has challenged the traditional genealogy of Santa Claus. "The usual explanation that Santa Claus 'came from' Saint Nicholas seems to be backward: Saint Nicholas was created to take the place of the heathen god"—the traditional "wild man" of pre-Christian cultures.[22]

As Siefker describes it, the "wild man" goes by many names in folk cultures: Jack or Robin or Beelzebub in the British Isles, Old Hornie or Donas on the Scottish coast, Ruprecht or Pelznichol in the German territories, Orcus in the Pyrenees mountains, Jass in Switzerland, Papa Bois in the

22. Siefker, *Last of the Wild Men*, 71.

Caribbean, Harlequin or the fool in Italy, and the goat-man in Greek festivals. According to what information we can gather from the most primitive artwork, poetry, festivals, and dramas, the "wild man" shuffled, snorted, leapt about, clanged bells, and threatened onlookers with a club, a branch, or a Yule log. His features were rough, as if he just emerged from the woods. He would be covered in soot, moss, greenery, or fur; his beard would be matted and brambly, his back bent and hunched. He represented civilization's opposite: the fickle mirth of the blossom, the mirthless ferocity of the rainstorm, the musky smell of damp humus, the moonfaced howl of virility.

At year's end, this wildness needed to be caught, chained, and killed so as to harness and direct the virile strength of nature into the fields and livestock of the people. For agricultural families whose very lives depended on the yield of the earth, who watched the skies for clouds and the soil for signs, who followed the phases of the moon and the cycles of the seasons, the drama was reenacted ritually, annually, and with blood-red conviction. It was repeated in a hundred local variations over the course of thousands of years.

The "wild man" stock-character is as old as the 30,000-year-old engraving of a man dressed in animal skins in the Caverne des Trois-Frères in France and as contemporary as Santa Claus, who also dresses in fur from his head to his feet, has a prominent beard, possesses magical powers, and makes an appearance at year's end. Santa Claus does not carry a club, but he does hold a whip for the reindeer. He has traded a hunched back for a sack of toys over his shoulder. He lives alone in the remote and uninhabitable North Pole instead of the impenetrable forest, but Siefker's argument is that he is the same basic character. According to Siefker, the identity of Saint Nicholas was used as a cloak for these "wild man" personas—of which Santa Claus is simply the latest incarnation. Saint Nicholas served to baptize and Christianize and ultimately preserve ancient folkways.

We do not have to accept the entirety of Siefker's world-encompassing thesis to acknowledge the truth of its observations. At times Nicholas can assume qualities of a minor divinity—a pre-Christian spirit of the season. How does this happen? One need only consider the history of the German Christkind to see the process in miniature. In the sixteenth century Martin Luther and the Lutherans attempted to replace Saint Nicholas and the other Christmas saints with Jesus Christ himself. The holy infant Christ was the one responsible for the mysterious Christmastide gifts. The Christkind or

"Christ-child" should be honored as the gift-giver, so Lutheran ministers taught, and not some other sprite or fairy or patron.

But from the start, Luther's pious aspirations unraveled as the Christ-kind character blended with the "wild man" types and tropes. For instance, at German parades, festivals, and processions, the Christkind, Christmann, or Christpuppe, although literally the "Christ child," was not impersonated by a baby in diapers. This was just impractical. Instead the part was played by a young girl in a billowing white robe with a golden crown and single white candle. She dispensed not only toys and sweets for good boys and girls but switches for the naughty ones. Along the French Alsace borders of Germany, Hans Trapp accompanied her. A shadowy bearded figure draped in bearskins, he menaced children with a heavy rod and was rumored to drag them off and eat them. And so, with little effort the "wild man" found his way back into Germanic folk practice, even after it had been Christian-ized with the name of Christ himself—Christkind.[23]

Saint Nicholas, when not himself performing the role of the "wild man," sometimes travels with a companion who functions as the "wild man" counterpart to his saintly and luminous self. This alter ego goes by many names: the harlequin Zwarte Piet in Dutch country, the furry and horned Krampus in Austria, and the dirty-brown Schmutzli in Switzerland. In France and Luxembourg he appears as a penitent friar, Père Fouettard, who acts more like "the bogeyman" or "the beater"—as his name indicates (*le fouet* is a whip, switch, scourge). In the Berchtesgaden region of Germany, the so-called Buttnmandl procession to this day features the stately Bishop Nicholas moving from house to house in the company of a of straw-and-fur–covered creatures ringing bells and chasing out bad spirits. A female companion to Saint Nicholas traveled for a time in Swabia and Augsburg under the name Berchtel or Buzebergt, and like the others, punished bad children with the rod and rewarded others with nuts and apples.[24] The "wild man" with all his (and her!) symbolic associations persist in many Saint Nicholas traditions.

---

23. Ibid., 158.

24. She also went by the name Budelfrau or Berchte. Miles, *Christmas in Ritual and Tradition*, 220.

Christmas and Commerce

In our own day the great machine of commerce has domesticated the wild man for consumer consumption. The Christkind, who is usually represented by a young female with blonde hair and dressed in white, is no longer known primarily for her nighttime travels and folklore activities. She is recognized for her connection to Christmas capitalism. At the opening ceremonies of the Christkindlesmarkt in Nürnberg, Germany, one of the most famous Christmas markets in the world, the Christkind's blessing officially opens the season of selling. In the United States, Santa Claus has likewise been contracted by big business to peddle products from Coca-Cola to lingerie to video games.

Christmas, Hanukah, Kwanza, and the other orbiting holidays of the season have been drawn into the vortex of spending and selling. Whether purchasing gifts or home decorations, buying holiday attire or party food, or simply browsing the festive department stores and malls, the season floats on a tide of holiday shopping. It begins with stampedes of in-store shoppers on Black Friday and online consumers on Cyber Monday and continues at a hyperventilated pace until it fizzles out in end-of-year clearance sales.

The complaint of concerned Christians about the commercialization of Christmas is nothing new. The cry against consumer culture and the carnage it inflicts upon the magical innocence of Christmas has been voiced many times. Lucy figured all this out years ago in Charlie Brown's animated Christmas special. "Look, Charlie, let's face it," she snaps. "We all know that Christmas is a big commercial racket. It's run by a big eastern syndicate, you know."[25] If Lucy's comments rung loud and clear back in 1965, so much more so today.

From the very start, Christmas, at least in the American setting, has been wedded to commercialism. Historian Gerry Bowler has found a flyer dating back to 1820 for a New York jewelry store featuring Saint Nicholas.[26] In the 1840s, H. W. Pease put the Christmas saint to use in his own advertising campaign of printed flyers and had the address of his Albany variety store inscribed on Saint Nicholas's basket of goodies. Ten years later Mr. Pease would introduce his customers to the first Christmas cards printed in America. In the 1870s merchants began to promote poinsettias as Christ-

---

25. *A Charlie Brown Christmas*, directed by Bill Melendez (1965).
26. Bowler, *Santa Claus*, 115.

mas novelties and in 1880 Woolworth's sold the first glass ornaments in the United States. Frank Woolworth, owner of the Lancaster, Pennsylvania store, initially expressed skepticism about the German trinkets. He feared that people would not buy them because they didn't *do* anything. To his delight and surprise, he sold out in a day.[27] Ever since, Christmas and its saints have been inextricably linked to the advertising industry and all its tentacles.

For some, this comes as dreadful news. Some conscientious pastors and commentators lament that commercialism ruins the meaning of Christmas. Some would even say that big business and insatiable consumer desire have broken Christmas beyond repair. I do not share this assessment. It is my firm belief that big business, consumerism, and greed can't wreck the meaning of Christmas because of the plain fact that Christmas does not depend on any of us for its meaning. Christmas finds its ultimate meaning, purpose, and truth in the birth of God's Son for the salvation of the world, and this is something that we can neither add to nor take away from.

The joy of the Lord simply invites us to participate in it.

Duty demands I bring this polar express to a halt. We have come to the end of our Christmas journey together. I have tried not to leave anything out. My aim has been to mix biblical, theological, historical, and cultural reflections into a fragrant Christmas potpourri. The tendency for many people is to separate and segment Christmas into different categories: here a book on the birth of Jesus, there a study of cultural traditions of Christmas. I wished to avoid the compartmentalizing urge. Christmas calls for deep conversation about the incarnation of the Word made flesh but it also calls to mind warm thoughts of family tradition. It invites meditation on the nativity narratives of Luke and Matthew and at the same time it allows indulgence in inflatable yard ornaments and gaudy Christmas sweaters. My design was not to deal with one or the other—*just* the biblical theology of the season or *just* the kitschy carnival of cultural celebration—but both, together.

I wanted this book to deal with all these experiences and convictions because Christmas hits us with everything at once—the spiritual, the practical, the silly, the financial, the scriptural, the familial, and the social. 'Tis the season to be jolly *and* reverent, to sing for joy *and* to contemplate in

27. "Christmas Decorations for Seven Generations," http://www.woolworthsmuseum.co.uk/xmasdecs.htm, accessed September 16, 2015.

silence, to lock arms with friends *and* to extend a hand to fellow human beings in need.

Works Cited

Ælred of Rievaulx. "Two Sermons for the Nativity of the Lord." Translated by Basil Cunningham. *Cistercian Studies Quarterly* 37.1 (February 2002) 83–89.

Albinus. *The Platonic Doctrines of Albinus.* Translated by Jeremiah Reedy. Grand Rapids: Phanes, 1991.

Alighieri, Dante. *The Divine Comedy of Dante Alighieri: Paradiso.* Vol. 3. Translated by Robert Durling. New York: Oxford University Press, 2011.

Allison, Dale. *The New Moses.* Minneapolis: Fortress, 1993.

Anderson, Felix Just, and Tom Thatcher, eds. *John, Jesus, and History, vol. 2: Aspects of Historicity in the Fourth Gospel.* Atlanta: SBL, 2009.

Anselm. *The Prayers and Meditations of St. Anselm.* Translated by Benedicta Ward. New York: Penguin, 1973.

Aquinas, Thomas. *Summa Theologiae.* Vol. 44 (2.2, 155–170). Edited by Thomas Gilby. Cambridge: Cambridge University Press, 2006.

Athanasius, *On the Incarnation.* Translated by John Behr. Yonkers, NY: St. Vladimir's Seminary Press, 2011.

Augustine. *De Genesi ad litteram. Patrologia Latina.* Vol. 34. Edited by J.-P. Migne. Paris: N.P., 1844–1855.

———. *The Enchiridion.* Translated by Bruce Harbert. Hyde Park, NY: New City, 1999.

———. *Sermons* III/6. Translated by Edmund Hill. New Rochelle, NY: New City, 1993.

———. *Sermons on the Liturgical Seasons.* Translated by Mary Muldowny. Fathers of the Church, vol. 38. Washington: The Catholic University of America Press, 1959.

———. *The Trinity.* Translated by Edmund Hill. Brooklyn, NY: New City, 1991.

Aune, David, ed. *The Gospel of Matthew in Current Study.* Grand Rapids: Eerdmans, 2001.

Bailey, Kenneth. *The Good Shepherd.* Downers Grove, IL: InterVarsity, 2014.

Bainton, Roland, ed. *Martin Luther's Christmas Book.* Minneapolis: Augsburg, 1997.

Balthasar, Hans Urs von. *Dare We Hope "That All Men Be Saved?"* San Francisco: Ignatius, 1988.

Barthel, Peter, and George van Kooten, eds. *The Star of Bethlehem and the Magi: Interdisciplinary Perspectives from Experts on the Ancient Near East, the Greco-Roman World, and Modern Astronomy.* Boston: Brill, 2015.

Basil. *Homily 27. Patrologia Graeca.* Vol. 31. Edited by J.-P. Migne. Paris: N.P., 1844–1855.

Benedict. *Saint Benedict's Rule*. Translated by Patrick Barry. Mahwah, NJ: Hidden Spring, 2004.

Bernard. *Sermons of St. Bernard on Advent and Christmas*. New York: Benziger, 1909.

———. *Homilies in Praise of the Blessed Virgin Mary*. Translated by Marie-Bernard Saïd. Kalamazoo, MI: Cistercian, 1993.

Bock, Darrell. *Luke 1:1–9:50*. Baker Exegetical Commentary of the New Testament. Grand Rapids: Baker, 1994.

Boguslawski, Alexander. *The Vitae of St. Nicholas and His Hagiographical Icons in Russia*. PhD diss., University of Kansas, 1980.

Book of Divine Prayers and Services of the Catholic Orthodox Church of Christ. New York: Blackshaw, 1938.

Bovon, François. *Luke 1:1–9:50*. Hermeneia. Minneapolis: Fortress, 2002.

Bowler, Gerry. *Santa Claus: A Biography*. Toronto: McClelland & Stewart, 2005.

Braaten, Carl, and Robert Jenson, eds. *Mary, Mother of God*. Grand Rapids: Eerdmans, 2004.

Brooks, Phillips. *O Little Town of Bethlehem*. New York: Holiday, 1907.

Brown, Peter. *Through the Eye of a Needle: Wealth, the Fall of Rome, and the Making of Christianity in the West*. Princeton, NJ: Princeton University Press, 2012.

Brown, Raymond. *Birth of the Messiah*. New York: Doubleday, 1977.

Cahill, Thomas. *A Saint on Death Row*. New York: Anchor, 2009.

Catechism of the Catholic Church. 2nd ed. Washington: United States Catholic Conference, 2011.

Cavanaugh, William. *Torture and Eucharist*. Malden, MA: Blackwell, 1998.

Chesterton, G. K. *Orthodoxy*. New York: Image, 2014.

Chrysostom, John. *In Kalendas*. Patrologia Graeca. Vol. 48. Edited by J.-P. Migne. Paris: N.P., 1844–1855.

Clement of Alexandria. *Christ the Educator*. Translated by Simon Wood. Fathers of the Church. Washington, DC: Catholic University of America Press, 1954.

———. *Stromateis: Books One to Three*. Translated by John Ferguson. Fathers of the Church. Washington, DC: Catholic University of America Press, 1991.

Cornell, Vincent. "Fruit of the Tree of Knowledge: The Relationship between Faith and Practice in Islam." In *The Oxford History of Islam*, edited by John Esposito, 63–106. New York: Oxford University Press, 1999.

Daniélou, Jean. *The Bible and the Liturgy*. Notre Dame, IN: University of Notre Dame Press, 1956.

da Todi, Jacopone. *Jacopone da Todi: The Lauds*. Translated by Serge and Elizabeth Hughes. New York: Paulist, 1981.

Davies, W. D., and Dale Allison. *The Gospel According to Saint Matthew*, vol. 1. International Critical Commentary. Edinburgh: T&T Clark, 1988.

Denzinger, Heinrich, ed. *Enchiridion Symbolorum*. 43rd ed. San Francisco: Ignatius, 2012.

Dio. *Roman History*. Vol. 4. Translated by Earnest Cary. Loeb Classical Library. Cambridge, MA: Harvard University Press, 1961.

Dionysius Exiguus. *Liber de Paschate*. Patrologia Latina. Vol. 67. Edited by J.-P. Migne. Paris: N.P., 1844–1855.

The Divine Liturgies of Our Holy Fathers John Chrysostom and Basil the Great. Pittsburgh: The Byzantine Catholic Metropolitan Church, 2006.

Éla, Jean-Marc. *My Faith as an African*. Translated by J. Brown and S. Perry. Maryknoll, NY: Orbis, 1988.

Erb, Peter, ed. *Pietists*. New York: Paulist, 1983.

English, Adam C. *The Saint Who Would Be Santa Claus*. Waco, TX: Baylor University Press, 2012.

Ephrem the Syrian. *Hymns*. Translated by Kathleen McVey. New York: Paulist, 1989.

———. *Hymns on Faith*. Translated by Jeffrey Wickes. Washington: Catholic University of America Press, 2015.

Eusebius, *Demonstratio evangelica*. Translated by W. J. Ferrar. London: SPCK, 1920.

———. *Historia Ecclesiastica/Eusebius: The Church History*. Translated by Paul Maier. Grand Rapids: Kregel, 1999, 2007.

Everitt, Anthony. *Augustus*. New York: Random House, 2007.

France, R. T. *The Gospel of Matthew*. New International Commentary on the New Testament. Grand Rapids: Eerdmans, 2007.

Freeman, Curtis. *Contesting Catholicity*. Waco, TX: Baylor University Press, 2014.

George, Paduthottu. *The Rod in the Old Testament*. Dehli: ISPCK, 2004.

Gutiérrez, Gustavo. *Theology of Liberation*. Maryknoll, NY: Orbis, 2001.

Graf, Fritz. "Fights about Festivals: Libanius and John Chrysostom on the *Kalendae Ianuariae* in Antioch." *Archiv für Religionsgeschichte* 13.1 (March 2012) 175–86.

Green, Joel. *Gospel of Luke*. New International Commentary on the New Testament. Grand Rapids: Eerdmans, 1997.

Gregory of Nazianzen. *Oratio* 38. *Patrologia Graeca*. Vol. 36. Edited by J.-P. Migne. Paris: N.P., 1844–1855.

Hagner, Donald. *Matthew 1–13*. Word Biblical Commentary 33A. Dallas: Word, 1993.

Hahn, Scott. *Joy to the World: How Christ's Coming Changed Everything (And Still Does)*. New York: Image, 2014.

Harper, Keith, ed. *Send the Light: Lottie Moon*. Macon, GA: Mercer University Press, 2002.

Herodotus. *Histories*. Loeb Classical Library vol. 117. Cambridge, MA: Harvard University Press, 1989.

Hoehner, H. W. *Chronological Aspects of the Life of Christ*. Grand Rapids: Zondervan, 1977.

Honorius of Autun. *In annunciatione Sancta Mariae*. *Patrologia Latina*. Vol. 172. Edited by J.-P. Migne. Paris: N.P., 1844–1855.

Huertz, Christopher. *Unexpected Gifts*. New York: Howard, 2013.

Hutton, Roland. *Stations of the Sun*. New York: Oxford University Press, 1996.

It's Fun to be a Real Santa Claus. Santa Claus, IN: Santa Claus Research Committee, 1956.

Jacobs, Harriet. *Incidents in the Life of a Slave Girl*. Originally published in Boston, 1861. Reprint. Cambridge: Cambridge University Press, 1987.

Jerome. *Commentary on Matthew*. Fathers of the Church. Washington: Catholic University of America Press, 2008.

———. *Dogmatic and Polemical Works*. Fathers of the Church vol. 53. Washington: Catholic University of America Press, 1965.

———. *Letters and Select Works*. Edited by Philip Schaff. Nicene and Post-Nicene Fathers 2.6. Grand Rapids: Eerdmans, 2005.

Johnson, A. C., et al., eds. *Ancient Roman Statutes*. Austin, TX: University of Texas Press, 1961.

Jones, Charles W. *The St. Nicholas Liturgy*. Berkeley, CA: University of California Press, 1963.

Josephus. *Jewish Antiquities*. Vols. 8 and 9. Translated by Ralph Marcus and Louis Feldman. Loeb Classical Library. Cambridge, MA: Harvard University Press, 1963, 1965.

Justin Martyr. *St. Justin Martyr: The First and Second Apologies*. Translated by Leslie Barnard. New York: Paulist, 1997.

Keener, Craig. *Gospel of John*. Vol. 1. Peabody, MA: Hendrickson, 2003.

Kelly, Joseph. *The Feast of Christmas*. Collegeville, MN: Liturgical, 2010.

———. *The Origins of Christmas*. Collegeville, MN: Liturgical, 2004.

Kraybill, Donald, Steven Nolt, and David Weaver-Zercher. *Amish Grace: How Forgiveness Transcended Tragedy*. San Francisco: Jossey-Bass, 2010.

Lactantius. *Divine Institutes*. Translated by Mary Francis McDonald. Fathers of the Church vol. 49. Washington, DC: Catholic University of America Press, 1964.

Lash, Nicholas. *Holiness, Speech and Silence*. Burlington, VT: Ashgate, 2004.

Leo the Great. *Sermons*. The Fathers of the Church vol. 93. Washington, DC: Catholic University of America Press, 1996.

Lincoln, Andrew. *Born of a Virgin? Reconceiving Jesus in the Bible, Tradition, and Theology*. Grand Rapids: Eerdmans, 2013.

Lindbeck, George. *The Nature of Doctrine*. Philadelphia: Westminster, 1984.

Lossky, Vladimir. *Mystical Theology of the Eastern Church*. Crestwood, NY: St Vladimir's Seminary Press, 1998.

Louth, Andrew. *Discerning the Mystery*. New York: Oxford University Press, 1983.

de Lubac, Henri. "Commentaire du preamble et du chapitre I." *La revelation divine*. Vol. 1. Edited by B-D Dupuy. Paris: Cerf, 1968.

———. *Exégèse Médiévale*. Vol. II.1. Paris: Aubier, 1961.

Lucian. *The Works of Lucian of Samosata*. 4 vols. Translated by H. W. Fowler and F. G. Fowler. Oxford: Clarendon, 1905.

Luijten, Eric. *Sacramental Forgiveness as a Gift of God*. Lueven: Peeters, 2003.

Luther, Marin. *Luther's Works: Sermons II*. Vol. 52. Edited by Hans Hillerbrand. Philadelphia: Fortress, 1974.

Maier, Paul. *The First Christmas: The True and Unfamiliar Story*. Grand Rapids: Kregel, 2001.

Marshak, Adam. *The Many Faces of Herod the Great*. Grand Rapids: Eerdmans, 2015.

Mather, Cotton. *Grace Defended: A Censure on the Ungodliness, By Which the Glorious Grace of God, Is Too Commonly Abused*. Boston: B. Green, 1712.

McClendon, James, and John H. Yoder. "Christian Identity in Ecumenical Perspective." *Journal of Ecumenical Studies* 27.3 (1990) 562–78.

Merton, Thomas. *Conjectures of A Guilty Bystander*. New York: Doubleday, 1966.

Meyers, Carol, and Toni Craven, eds. *Women in Scripture: A Dictionary of Named and Unnamed Women*. Grand Rapids: Eerdmans, 2000.

Milbank, John. *Being Reconciled*. New York: Routledge, 2003.

———. *Theology and Social Theory*. Cambridge: Blackwell, 1993.

Miles, Clement. *Christmas in Ritual and Tradition*. New York: Dover, 1976.

Molnar, Michael. *The Star of Bethlehem: The Legacy of the Magi*. Piscataway, NJ: Rutgers University Press, 1999.

More, Thomas. *Utopia*. Rockville, MD: Arc Manor, reprint 2008.

Mosshammer, Alden. *The Easter Computus and the Origins of the Christian Era*. New York: Oxford University Press, 2008.

Mulder, John, and Morgan Roberts. *28 Carols to Sing at Christmas*. Eugene, OR: Cascade, 2015.

Myers, Ched. *Binding the Strong Man*. Maryknoll, NY: Orbis, 2008.

Nietzsche, Friedrich. *The Gay Science.* Translated by Walter Kaufmann. New York: Vintage, 1974.

Nissenbaum, Stephen. *The Battle for Christmas.* New York: Vintage, 1996.

O'Toole, Robert. *Luke's Presentation of Jesus: A Christology.* Rome: Editrice Pontificio Istituto Biblico, 2008.

Origen. *Contra Celsum.* Translated by Henry Chadwick. Cambridge: Cambridge University Press, 1953.

de Paola, Tomie. *The Legend of Old Befana.* Orlando: Voyager, 1980.

Pliny. *Natural History.* Vol. 1. Translated by H. Rackham. Loeb Classical Library. Cambridge, MA: Harvard University Press, 1958.

Potter, David. *Constantine the Emperor.* New York: Oxford University Press, 2012.

Price, S. R. F. *Rituals and Power: The Roman Imperial Cult in Asia Minor.* Cambridge: Cambridge University Press, 1984.

Protoevangelium of James. In *Lost Scriptures*, edited by Bart Ehrman, 63–72. New York: Oxford University Press, 2003.

Ratzinger, Joseph (Pope Benedict XVI). *Jesus of Nazareth: From the Baptism in the Jordan to the Transfiguration.* Translated by Adrian Walker. San Francisco: Ignatius, 2007.

———. *Jesus of Nazareth: The Infancy Narratives.* Translated by Adrian Walker. San Francisco: Ignatius, 2012.

Restad, Penne. *Christmas in America: A History.* New York: Oxford University Press, 1995.

Robinson, John M. *An Introduction to Early Greek Philosophy.* Boston: Houghton Mifflin, 1968.

Roll, Susan. *Toward the Origins of Christmas.* Netherlands: Kok Pharos, 1995.

Saward, John. *Cradle of Redeeming Love: The Theology of the Christmas Mystery.* San Francisco: Ignatius, 2002.

———. *Redeemer in the Womb: Jesus Living in Mary.* San Francisco: Ignatius, 1993.

Schäfer, Peter. *Jesus in the Talmud.* Princeton, NJ: Princeton University Press, 2007.

Schürer, Emil. *A History of the Jewish People in the Time of Jesus Christ.* Vol. 1. Translated by J. Macpherson. New York: Scribner, 1890.

Siefker, Phyllis. *Santa Claus, Last of the Wild Men.* Jefferson, NC: McFarland, 2006.

Suetonius. *Augustus.* Loeb Classical Library. Cambridge, MA: Harvard University Press, 1913.

Sullivan, Regina. *Lottie Moon.* Baton Rouge: Louisiana State University Press, 2011.

Sulpicius Severus. *Vita S. Martini.* Translated by Caroline White. New York: Penguin, 1998.

Tacitus. *The Annals.* Translated by John Yardley. New York: Oxford University Press, 2008.

Thatcher, Tom, ed. *What We Have Heard from the Beginning: The Past, Present and Future of Johannine Studies.* Waco, TX: Baylor University Press, 2007.

Thomas of Celano. *Lives of St. Francis of Assisi.* Translated by A. G. Ferrers Howell. London: Methuen and Co., 1908.

Thurman, Howard. *Jesus and the Disinherited.* Boston: Beacon, 1976.

Torrance, Thomas F. *Incarnation: The Person and Life of Christ.* Downers Grove: IVP Academic, 2008.

von Bingen, Hildegard. *Symphonia: A Critical Edition of the Symphonia armonie celestium revelationum.* Edited by Barbara Newman. Ithaca, NY: Cornell University Press, 1989.

Ware, Kallistos. *The Orthodox Way.* Crestwood, NY: St. Vladimir's Seminary Press, 1999.

Willimon, William H., and Stanley Hauerwas. *Lord, Teach Us.* Nashville: Abingdon, 1996.

WORKS CITED

Yoder, John Howard. *The Priestly Kingdom: Social Ethics as Gospel.* Notre Dame, IN: University of Notre Dame Press, 1984.

Made in the USA
Columbia, SC
14 December 2021

51396950R00107